MAY YOU KNOW IT TO BE TRUE

Exhortations by

DENNIS GILLETT

THE CHRISTADELPHIAN
404 SHAFTMOOR LANE
HALL GREEN
BIRMINGHAM B28 8SZ

First Edition 2003
Reprinted 2007

ISBN 978-085189157-6

Printed in England by:
The Cromwell Press Ltd
Trowbridge
Wiltshire

FOREWORD

THIS collection of exhortations has been compiled from the legacy of typewritten scripts left by the late Brother Dennis Gillett, who fell asleep in the Lord in November 1992. The notes were used by him almost verbatim when delivering his addresses, and only occasionally has it been necessary to fill them out. It is hoped that any insertions fit in seamlessly and remain faithful to the original thoughts and style.

Of course, his inimitable style is a large factor in making these exhortations what they are, but by no means the most significant. If we were to place them by rank, then first must be the depth of knowledge of God's word, followed by the spiritual perception that is evident throughout this book. The homely, personal style is then used to great effect in bringing spiritual truths to the reader. Brother Dennis deftly puts his finger on the issues which matter and conveys them in a way that demands a response in the heart of the disciple of Christ.

An example of his humorous way of bringing home practical lessons is found in the introduction to "Redeeming the Time" (page 99): "When you think about it, living the life of faith is really about the right use of time. It is stating the obvious, but everybody has to do something with time. Indolent people waste it, busy people save it, bored people kill it, conductors beat it, musicians keep it, railway trains lose it—disciples are urged to redeem it". Brother Dennis, having captured our attention, then goes on to explain the practical and spiritual issues involved in 'redeeming' time.

Many of the exhortations end with stirring words of confident assurance and eternal hope. Despite his own self-confessed weaknesses, Brother Dennis was clearly moved by these thoughts in his own life, and it was his desire to share his experiences of peace and joy with his hearers. Many an exhortation concluded with the prayer, "God grant that in your deepest heart *you may know it to be true*". To avoid duplication, some of these concluding prayers have been removed from this collection, but the heartfelt desire that we might know these things is still evident throughout.

Each exhortation is based on a chapter of scripture, some extensively, others just on a verse or phrase taken from that chapter. The relevant chapters are detailed, so that an exhortation may be readily used with the Daily Readings for a personal breaking of bread. There are in some cases several other chapters that would be appropriate. The book is ordered by the chapter to which each exhortation is primarily related.

This compilation will be helpful to many who need encouragement to follow Christ in everyday things. Bible study should always lead to a practical response, and true exhortation requires us to consider our hearts. Indeed, on the odd occasion when Brother Dennis felt he was drifting towards an academic exposition, he would pull himself up as in the following example: "Now no doubt the question in your minds is this: where in this rather Bible-Class-style study is the exhortational element? What is the message we may take away today to help us in the coming week?" Then, after speaking in terms of personal application, he concludes: "Here is the word of encouragement. Get back to this holy word of God. Let it become incarnate in your consciousness. Discover anew that enigmatic but loving Christ: a human life so real, so definite, so divine, so warm, so tender, so actual, so unique, that we are compelled to cry with Thomas, 'My Lord and my God'".

Those who were close to Brother Dennis tell us that his faith was intensely practical. He was ever first to visit, console and encourage. Any task he undertook would be completed enthusiastically and painstakingly. He would always leave time for a smile. Our consolation is that "the man of Nazareth", "the man of Galilee", "the man of the seamless robe", the man whom Brother Dennis loved and served right up to the end, is surely not long to remain away.

COLIN WALTON
BIRMINGHAM 2003

CONTENTS

1

THE PRIESTLY BENEDICTION (NUMBERS 6)

YOU may have deduced already that this exhortation is based upon the last six verses of Numbers 6. These words are very familiar to us as we often use them at baptismal services. But that is not the only way in which they can be used and it seemed to me that it might be profitable to look at them again by way of exhortation. The reason is this: the priestly benediction which was once and originally pronounced upon Israel in a wonderful and profound way, has also been pronounced upon you. Read verse 27 as a beginning:

> "And they shall put my name upon the children of Israel; and I will bless them."

Notice that the blessings come to Israel by this ancient formula in association with the putting on of the name of God—as though the meaning of the name is fulfilled in the threefold form of the benediction.

The Name of God

I am sure that this is not the right place for a treatise on the name of God. It is a subject very dear to many Christadelphians and of very great interest. It is clear that the name of *Yahweh* came to have among the Hebrew people a greater sanctity than any other name, so much so that they would not utter the sounds of the word—it was not to be pronounced. Men of God do not have that same reticence today; they use the name regularly and often. I want to say nothing about *Elohim*, *El Shaddai*, *Adonai*—as I say, it is an interesting subject for another occasion, but not now. Notwithstanding, there is one name which I would like to draw your attention to because it does relate to Numbers 6 in a real way.

The name was revealed to Moses at the burning bush—in the Hebrew, *Eyheh Asher Eyheh*:

> "And God said unto Moses, I AM THAT I AM: and he said, Thus shalt thou say unto the children of Israel, I AM hath sent me unto you." (Exodus 3:14)

Now the point is this: those who are experts in Hebrew explain to us that the real intention of the words is not so much "*I am*", but "*I will be*". So the name is "*I will be what I will be*". In other words God is revealed as a 'becoming' God—"I will be" suggests that. "I am" and "I will be": here we have an all-sufficient God active on behalf of others; the adaptation of God's being to the necessity of men.

God 'becoming'

God is a 'becoming' God, becoming all that His people need by way of redemption, salvation and protection. Years before, men found the meaning of the name in the experience of God without fully understanding it. Abraham once said "*Jehovah Jireh*"—'the becoming one sees and provides'. So it is then in Numbers 6 we see God blessing His people in the most real sense; that is becoming to them all they need in the hour of faithfulness and failure. I use the words *faithfulness* and *failure* quite deliberately, because as the mind roves over the movement of God's people through the centuries, as we ponder the Old Testament, we are aware that Yahweh is a God always becoming what His people need. Let me illustrate. In the hour of their unutterable folly He became fiery judgement; in the hour of their repentance He became a God of great compassion; when the billows broke upon them He was as a mighty fortress; when their heart was weary and sad, He, the God of the stellar spaces, came very close to them and looked into their broken hearts. In all their afflictions He was afflicted. In their failure and distress, always underneath were the everlasting arms, as Moses confessed.

Then at last, in the fullness of time, the great truth about the name of God sang itself out in mystic wonder: the Word became flesh and tabernacled among the Galilean fishermen. The "I am" of essential being became the "I am" which stoops and bends and gives—the becoming one, the fullness of glory and the fullness of grace. So the grace of God was at last sounded in human history in the simplest of all names: Jesus—Joshua—God's salvation. Humanity is touched without being crushed but blessed. And in the benediction the name is revealed and there is healing and help for all broken souls.

The Priestly Benediction

With this in mind then, come back to the priestly benediction. I am careful to say 'priestly benediction' because I want to remind you that the priestly office has two features. Essentially the priestly office is mediatorial and the two features are firstly intercessory and secondly benedictory. In addition, each of these features has two functions. As an intercessor the priest stands in the presence of God pleading the cause of men and then he stands in the presence of men pleading the cause of God. In the act of benediction he stands in the presence of men pronouncing the blessings of God, and then stands in the presence of God offering the praises of men. In this little exhortation I am concerned chiefly with the second aspect of his work—that is the benediction or the pronouncement of the divine blessing upon the people of God.

This was a very real and distinct part of the worship of the Hebrew people. In Leviticus 9 you will find this at verse 22:

> "And Aaron lifted up his hand toward the people, and blessed them, and came down from offering of the sin offering, and the burnt offering, and the peace offerings".

It is evident from this that in the order of the liturgy of Israel the pronouncement of the benediction followed the completion of the presentation of the offerings. This is right and what we might expect. Sin must first be dealt with and then the priest may say, "The LORD bless thee, and keep thee". Dedication now having been accomplished, the priest may say, "The LORD make his face shine upon thee, and be gracious unto thee". Peace having been established between men and God, the priest is able to say, "The LORD lift up his countenance upon thee, and give thee peace". One is a divinely natural consequence of the other.

Mark then the arrangement of Numbers 6. It is about a man who has separated himself to the Lord in a special and significant way; that is a man who through the priest makes offerings to God in confirmation of his separation. The chapter then closes with the priest moving from his function of intercession to his function of benediction:

> "And the LORD spake unto Moses, saying, Speak unto Aaron and unto his sons, saying, On this wise ye shall bless the children of Israel, saying unto them, The LORD bless thee, and keep thee: The LORD make his face shine upon thee, and be gracious unto thee: The LORD lift up his countenance upon thee, and give thee peace. And they shall put my name upon the children of Israel; and I will bless them." (verses 22–27)

Observe finally that as a result of the separation and the offerings and the benediction, the name of God is pronounced upon the people: "they shall put my name upon the children of Israel".

Separated unto the Lord

I need hardly stress the significance of all this to those in Christ—a people who have separated themselves unto the God of Israel in a very special sense. Consequently the blessing has been pronounced upon them by the high priest of the universe. The realisation of the blessing is the experience of salvation, common to each soul—even now, within the limitations of failing human life—and then without restriction through the spaciousness of eternal life. So the name of God has been put upon them in the most real sense. They bear the name of the Redeemer; they are his next of kin. Observe how the priestly benediction reveals the inclusive suggestiveness of the great name.

"The LORD bless thee ..."

Let us try to interpret the sentences of the benediction. "The LORD bless thee ...". The literal meaning of the phrase "bless thee" is rather startling. It means 'kneel to thee in order to serve'. I know it sounds strange but I will seek to show how this meaning emerges in actual practice. In 2 Chronicles chapters 5 and 6 there is a record of the ark being brought into the new temple. In 6:3 we find that Solomon blessed all the house of Israel and then added, "Blessed be the LORD God of Israel." He was blessing Israel and he was blessing God. But notice what he did: Solomon "kneeled down upon his knees before all the congregation of Israel, and spread forth his hands toward heaven" (verse 13). See how to the Hebrews this idea of blessing had in it the need to kneel and serve. Again in Psalm 95:

> "O come, let us worship and bow down: let us kneel before the LORD our maker. For he is our God; and we are the people of his pasture ...". (verses 6,7)

"Let us kneel" has in it the idea of 'Let us bless the LORD'. So although it may sound inappropriate when applied to God, it emerges as recognisable when you think of the group of men in the upper room and one of them girded with a towel is kneeling to wash their feet. So "The LORD bless thee" means 'may He place all He has at your disposal so that you may be cleansed, healed and saved'—God stooping and bending to succour men.

"And keep thee" means 'hedge thee about so as to protect thee'. In harmony with what we have said already about the 'becoming' God, it means God becoming all that His people need by way of providential care and prudential love. The incomprehensible becomes comprehensible. The God of the stellar spaces is looking into the face of any man or woman in need of succour and salvation, ready to heal and restore. He is not distant, light years away. He is nigh thee, closer than breath. So in the first stanza of the benediction we find ground for faith, confidence for hope, inspiration for love: "The LORD bless thee, and keep thee".

"The LORD make his face shine ..."

Then, "The LORD make his face shine upon thee, and be gracious unto thee". Notice that the shining face of God and His graciousness are related. The New Testament says we have seen the shining of God's glory in the face of Jesus Christ. It means that the face of God becomes luminous through Jesus Christ, and so the wonder of His grace becomes operative. It means that men, who left to themselves would be paralysed and would utterly fail, are reclaimed and remade, brought from darkness into marvellous light, irradiated and enlightened.

"The LORD lift up his countenance ..."

And then, "The LORD lift up his countenance upon thee". In these sentences there is no difference between the word "face" and the word "countenance": "the LORD make his *face* shine"; "the LORD lift up his *countenance*"—the same word. You will notice the difference in the fact that in the first, the face shines, and in the second it is lifted up. Now the essential idea of "lifting upon thee" is that of personal recognition. The separated man is recognised by the great God of heaven. A man who has lost his sense of nearness and has lost his sense of self-respect, may find that God has sought him, found him and recognised him, and the divine countenance has been turned towards him in compassion and tenderness.

The Lord is revealed not only as a means of blessing but also as a channel of blessing. Two men in the New Testament illustrate it. Zacchaeus at Jericho, a man who was despised and who had lost his self-respect, was in the tree and suddenly the Redeemer was underneath looking up and saying "Zacchaeus come down, I must stay with you today"—an act of personal recognition. The other is Peter in the court of the high priest. The Lord turned and looked upon him. It was a look of infinite pity and tenderness, fraught with love. Peter goes out weeping and is saved. The Lord lifted up his countenance upon him and there was grace to help in time of need.

"And give thee peace"

So to the final phrase: "And give thee peace". This is a revelation. Not only is Yahweh the source of blessing, not only the channel of blessing, but at last the very experience of blessing in the soul. Peace after all is essentially something you experience inwardly: "Let the peace of God rule in your hearts" says the Apostle Paul. For the man who receives the benediction there is a sense of relief and calm. A man under sentence of death has been pardoned; a man without hope has received assurance—his faith cancels his fear. He may lie down tonight and not be afraid. His heart is fixed trusting in the Lord.

These then were the priestly words committed unto Aaron to be pronounced upon a separated and pardoned people, and wherein the meaning of the name of God was confined and whereby it was put upon all who heard and received the benediction. So in this solemn moment we must remember once again that the one great inclusive blessing and the covering name of salvation are given to men by the sacrifice and priesthood of Jesus Christ. Now he alone has the power to pronounce it upon those who come confessing their need, willing to submit to his will and ready to claim him as their only daysman. So let us come this day, my brethren, to our true high priest, our advocate, to the "I am" who bends and stoops and becomes to his people all they need, both now and forever.

2

THE UNTRODDEN WAY
(JOSHUA 1)

THIS little exhortation has been extracted from the opening chapters of the book of Joshua. As a start it invites you to consider those people who stood on the perimeter of the promised land ready to cross the River Jordan into a new life. Quite evidently they are very different people from ourselves, far removed from us both in time and circumstance—and yet there are certain parallels between our situation and theirs which might make this exhortation worthwhile. Underlying these parallels are certain principles, which because they are perpetual in application, immediately become pertinent for us.

At the Border of the Land

Think of the people of God on the margin of a new land and a new life. First of all there are two things about them we must remember. They were a people very different in spirit from those who stood on the border of the good land forty years before at Kadesh Barnea. They had learned a great deal about themselves in the long interval. The wilderness experience had brought them face to face with the truth. They had discovered themselves and God in the strange processes of the journey. In the extremity and in the succour was unveiled the purpose of the experience. Let us remind ourselves what exactly that purpose was. I bring you to the word of Moses:

> "All the commandments which I command thee this day shall ye observe to do, that ye may live, and multiply, and go in and possess the land which the LORD sware unto your fathers. And thou shalt remember all the way which the LORD thy God led thee these forty years in the wilderness, to humble thee, and to prove thee, to know what was in thine heart, whether thou wouldest keep his commandments, or no. And he humbled thee, and suffered thee to hunger, and fed thee with manna, which thou knewest not, neither did thy fathers know; that he might make thee know that man doth not live by bread only, but by every

> word that proceedeth out of the mouth of the LORD doth man live." (Deuteronomy 8:1–3)

Observe the mystery and the wonder of God's method. Can I remind you of Deuteronomy 1:2: "There are eleven days' journey from Horeb by the way of mount Seir unto Kadesh Barnea"? Imagine that—eleven days' journey, which somehow took forty years. That is the mysterious method. He led them circuitously so that at last they would get straight. He delayed them in the wilderness so as to speed them into the good land.

When Moses uses the word 'prove'—"to prove thee"—it does not mean that God was needing to find out what was in them for He knew that already, but He wanted them to find out what they were in themselves. He wanted to make them to be outwardly what they were inwardly. So they learned a great deal about themselves and God.

A Time of Change

The other thing we must remember is that this was a time of change. The wilderness was behind them, the new life before them. The old leader was dead and Joshua had taken his place. The symbols of God's presence for so long had now gone; the fire and the cloud were no longer in their midst. Instead, the ark was the new sign which they were to follow. Before, they had waited for the moving of the cloud; now they were to wait for the moving of the ark and the priests. What Moses could not do, Joshua was certainly to do. Remember Joshua 1:2: "Moses my servant is dead; now therefore arise, go over this Jordan ...". The death of Moses was a turning point. A new era began for the people of God, and the new era brought new responsibilities. We could call that 'new accountability'—the responsibilities of expectation. It means that from the story on the pages of the Old Testament, we may gather light for that which lies ahead—the responsibilities of anticipation.

"Ye have not passed this way heretofore"

Notice then what Joshua said to the people as they made ready to cross Jordan:

> "And they commanded the people, saying, When ye see the ark of the covenant of the LORD your God, and the priests the Levites bearing it, then ye shall remove from your place, and go after it. Yet there shall be a space between you and it, about two thousand cubits by measure: come not near unto it, that ye may know the way by which ye must go: for ye have not passed this way heretofore." (Joshua 3:3,4)

When men set out on an untrodden pathway they cannot help being aware of the uncertainty. They knew some things about the good land. They knew it doubtless from the reports of the spies who had come back 40 years before—the reports preserved and no doubt repeated many times. They knew it from the words of Moses, in one of the finest pieces of poetry in the Bible:

> "... a good land, a land of brooks of water, of fountains and depths that spring out of valleys and hills; a land of wheat, and barley, and vines, and fig trees and pomegranates; a land of oil olive, and honey; a land wherein thou shalt eat bread without scarceness ...".
>
> (Deuteronomy 8:7–9)

It was true that they knew this but there was a great deal they did not know. They did not know what lay between them and the good land, so Joshua said: "Ye have not passed this way heretofore". They were aware therefore of the uncertainty of the future. There may be in some way a fascination in facing the unknown. There is always the possibility of something better—very often the cry of hope comes singing out of the unknown. Remember Rudyard Kipling's words:

> "Something hidden. Go and find it.
> Go and look behind the Ranges—
> Something lost behind the Ranges.
> Lost and waiting for you. Go!" *The Explorer*

Facing an Unknown Future

Out of the unknown the passion of discovery and realisation is born. Yes there is fascination in facing the future, even though it is unknown. But with the fascination there is also fear. There is the new opportunity, there is the promise and the possibility—but there is the opposition and the danger. We cannot tell how deep the river may prove to be, how tortuous the road, how many foes may lurk in the way. Their strength and their method is not known to us and therefore the danger is multiplied. So it was with these people on the margin of the new land. They knew the perils of the wilderness, and they had got used to them and met them. If you are accustomed to the peril it is robbed of half its power. It is the unknown that brings the fear. "Ye have not passed this way heretofore": it is strange and it is new and the anxiety arises out of a doubt that we are able to meet and vanquish the foes that lie ahead.

Take no Thought for the Morrow

Mark then the fascination and the fear, and consider this: that for the wise man there is value in both. Notice what Joshua said to those people encamped by the river: "Sanctify yourselves: for tomorrow the LORD will do wonders among you" (Joshua 3:5). What he meant was, 'Tomorrow is the Lord's, therefore today is for you, because you cannot see tomorrow'. In the very uncertainty there is the value that it compels men of faith and men of vision to grasp the forces which will make them equal to the things of tomorrow. If I am to march amongst precipices, be in the midst of ambush foes, surrounded by terrain which is strange and unknown, facing mystery and uncertainty by taking one step at a time and one day at a time—then sanctified common sense compels me to be equipped and fortified for the journey.

I almost hesitate to make a direct parallel at this stage between those people and ourselves, save to say that we do not know what lies between us and the Kingdom of God. I do not know how many victorious Jerichos there may be or how many disappointments like Ai. But you and I ought to be deeply conscious of the responsibilities of anticipation.

Grasping the Certainties

In the face of the uncertainty I think we are entitled, nay constrained, to ask, what are the certainties that we may grasp and take with us on the journey? First of all go back and hear a word of Moses as he came to the end of his leadership and as the people turned to face the new circumstances and the new experience. He charged them:

> "Thou shalt remember all the way which the LORD thy God led thee these forty years in the wilderness."
>
> (Deuteronomy 8:2)

This is one of the great certainties of life—the past. It is fixed and irreparable, and to the man of faith it is like a covert from the tempest, as the rivers of water in a dry place, as the shadow of a great rock in a weary land. Why? Because past deliverance predicts future deliverance; past succour promises future succour; past guidance predicates future guidance. This is what I mean. There is a river before us—how shall it be crossed? Measure the problem by the Red Sea. The water was divided and it can be divided again. There is an unknown land before us—how shall we find our way? Measure the unknown land by the unknown wilderness. He who led once can lead again. There is a new country and how shall we be sustained? Measure the coming hunger by the past manna and the past water. Remembrance of the past generates hope for the future. So, as you face tomorrow, let nobody take away from you the certainty of yesterday—and there are those who would: the scoffers who say, "Where is thy God?"

Draw Strength from Past and Present

They may confuse us about the *problems* of next year, but let them not confuse us about the *solutions* of last year. We were led in the great and terrible wilderness; in the hour of extremity He was there—the great Yahweh. No bread—and it rained from heaven. No water—and the flint gushed out. No certain way in the dreary wilderness and He went out before and found the places of rest. We sang a song on the safe side of the great Red Sea: it was a baptismal hymn. Let nobody frighten you with a running river. Never doubt your own experience. If you know what He is like, this great God, in the crises and the commonplaces of life, cling to that. Think of the day when the bitterest waters were sweetened; think of the day when you came to Elim and found rest. Think on it, and make it your inspiration. It is one of the great certainties as we go into the unknown.

The second great certainty is the present. Think what it was to these people on the verge of the new adventure. In their midst the living presence of God was focussed in the ark and in Joshua. The cloud and Moses were the wilderness symbols but now God was changing His method. Hitherto they had followed the cloud; now they were to follow the word of the Lord. It was the great certainty of the present: the voice of God, articulate, supreme—the voice of origination, speaking and directing. A living word and a living leader—these were the certainties of the present for them.

Certainties in Christ

I need hardly press the parallel; indeed to explain it to those so well tutored in the word of God would seem almost to insult you. For us there is the word of God, spoken and made incarnate and these are the certainties of the present, "that ye may know the way by which ye must go: for ye have not passed this way heretofore" (Joshua 3:4). But as we make the comparison a great contrast is revealed: that boy who was born in the backyard of an inn, amid the straw, under the dull lantern's light—they called him Joshua (Jehoshua, Numbers 13:16). He was surnamed first in heaven: "thou shalt call his name JESUS (Joshua): for he shall save his people from their sins". What the first great Joshua could never do, the second great Joshua has done once for all. The writer of Hebrews says that Joshua could not give them rest, and the reason he could not give them rest was because he could not deal with their sins (Hebrews 4:8). Jesus has taken away our sin and is now able to proclaim, "Come unto me, all ye that labour and are heavy laden, and I will give you rest". "He is able to save them to the uttermost that come unto God by him, seeing he ever liveth to make intercession for them". He is the one who leads out, and leads in and gives rest. This is the certainty of the present.

Future Certainties

Think of the final certainty—the future. Forgive the paradox. The uncertain future holds the greatest certainty of all. You know in your deepest heart that things for which you are longing are the surest things of all. There is an old saying, "Tomorrow never comes", and yet tomorrow is the greatest and most real thing of all, if by "tomorrow" we mean God's good land. The future is yours. In your inmost soul you feel the lure of the days which are to come. All things are yours. There is no power on earth which can defeat the purpose of God. "Ye have not passed this way heretofore"—but there comes singing up through your very nature the cry for life eternal. How will you face the future? I must lead you back to the word of God in Joshua 1:

> "I will not fail thee, nor forsake thee. Be strong and of a good courage." (verses 5,6)

It is a word for the man who struggles up after his fall, who strives on in spite of failure, who clings somehow to the belief that the victory will be won. The same conviction may be ours in Christ who cannot fail—as Peter gave testimony:

> "Humble yourselves therefore under the mighty hand of God, that he may exalt you in due time: casting all your care upon him; for he careth for you." (1 Peter 5:6,7)

His love is set on ruined men, to save them and to remake them.

"The LORD will do wonders among you"

So then, as we ponder this passage in the Old Testament, mark the responsibilities of anticipation: "Sanctify yourselves: for tomorrow the LORD will do wonders among you". Sanctify yourselves. In relation to the past, remember it and make it the inspiration of today. In relation to the present, maintain holy reverence for the word of God and undeviating loyalty to the living leader. In relation to the future, inspired by the past and empowered by the present, go into the untrodden pathway with faith to possess, and overcome.

Walled cities—take them; giants—slay them; difficulties—master them. Be strong and of good courage.

May God grant that in this solemn moment of bread breaking when you ponder these things in the presence of the Redeemer and sanctify yourselves, that in your deepest heart you may feel them to be true.

3

"WORSHIP THE LORD IN THE BEAUTY OF HOLINESS" (1 CHRONICLES 16)

THE theme of this exhortation is taken from 1 Chronicles 16, from that great psalm which David sang when the ark of God was brought up from the house of Obed-Edom to its resting place prepared in the tabernacle. David appealed to the people to praise God, calling upon them to recognise His glory, to think of His power and majesty. He urged them to respond to the things they were witnessing that day, and to answer the feelings in their hearts by praising God. "And all the people said, Amen, and praised the LORD." Now in that wonderful song, I wish to lay stress upon one stanza contained in verse 29, and in that stanza, one sentence:

> "Give unto the LORD the glory due unto his name: bring an offering, and come before him: *worship the LORD in the beauty of holiness*."

That is the sentence—a sentence containing two great Bible words: "worship" and "holiness"; and those two words are linked to yet another, which is in a sense strange, unusual in this context and provoking: the word is "beauty".

The word which is translated "beauty" occurs only five times in the scriptures: in Proverbs 14:28, where it is translated "honour" in the AV and "glory" in the RV; in 2 Chronicles 20:21, where King Jehoshaphat, going out to meet the Ammonites, arranges the singers to precede the soldiers and charges them in their songs to "praise the beauty of holiness"; in Psalm 29:2, 96:9 and in 1 Chronicles 16. It will be seen, therefore, that it is a rare word in the scriptures and used in the context of this great psalm of David in respect of worship, I hope to show it to be a significant word from which there is a lesson to be learned.

"Worship"

To come to that lesson we shall need first to consider the two other great words in the sentence: "worship" and "holiness". Dwell for a moment on the word worship'. In its first and deepest definition it means 'prostration'. It means bowing low and walking out backwards—as one did in recognition of the supremacy of the throne. It means yielding to authority, not out of fear but out of reverence. In the Bible, worship is the recognition that man is incomplete in every sense save as he is brought into relationship with God. So this realisation compels an attitude of worship and results in a trembling at His word and a glad and trusting submission to His will. The figure is that of a sheep that follows the leading of the shepherd and rests content in the pasturage which the shepherd appoints.

There are two words in the Bible which express the highest idea of worship: "Hallelujah" and "Amen". The first means 'Praise the Lord'. The second means 'Verily, so be it': it expresses agreement and submission. Both expressions occur in 1 Chronicles 16: "And all the people said, *Amen*, and *praised the LORD*" (verse 36). In Revelation 19 there is a vision of a great multitude saying "Hallelujah", and then a great responsive answer "Amen" (verses 1–4)—Amen to His will, and praise to His name. This is worship: not the mere boisterous shouting of the word by a half-enlightened man, but the quiet response of the heart realising the perfection and the absolute sufficiency of God.

See then that though the outward acts of worship are important, they are but secondary. The psalms and the anthems and readings are only worship if behind them we have learned to say "Amen" in our lives, and if our conduct is a silent "Hallelujah" to His praise. If I have not been worshipping God for six days, I shall have difficulty in worshipping today. The "Amen" will be empty if there is no corresponding submission in my life. The song will be a discord if there is no melody in my living. We sing and pray intermittently, but worship in its real sense is perpetual. It could be that the worship of our meeting is meaningless, unless it is preceded and prepared for by the worship of our daily living. That is the music which glorifies God.

"Holiness"

Dwell now on the word "holiness". If we were to say that holiness is righteousness, I think we should not be speaking the whole truth. I suggest that there is a distinction to be drawn between the two. In Luke 1, Zacharias spoke of God having "raised up an horn of salvation for us in the house of his servant David", whereby God would "grant unto us, that we being delivered out of the hand of our enemies might serve him without fear, in holiness *and* righteousness before him, all the days of our life" (verses 69,74,75).

In Ephesians 4:24, we read of "the new man, which after God is created in righteousness *and* true holiness". The distinction is this: righteousness is rightness of conduct; holiness is rightness of character. They are complementary, but there is a distinction. Holiness describes being; righteousness describes doing. So righteousness of life could issue from holiness of character. I say *could*, because when a man does right acts it does not follow necessarily that he is holy. Men can do right things out of self-respect. Men can do right things out of a high sense of duty. But sooner or later, under the stress and strain of temptation these motives may break down. Subtle temptation, some alluring advantage, will cause a man who for a long time has done right things, to turn to that which is untrue and mean and low.

This happens sometimes in very good people, and we cannot understand it. It may be that the explanation lies in this: they had rightness of conduct, but had never come to holiness. Holiness is not just a punctilious performance of certain virtues, or an abstemious refusal of vices. It is an approximation to the character of God: "Be ye holy, for I am holy"; "Be ye therefore perfect, even as your Father which is in heaven is perfect". That is not to say that holiness demands a condition of perfection. A man may not be perfect at the circumference, but if he is holy he will be right at the centre. Holiness sometimes means serving God faithfully in small ways and not minding that they are so small. If we are really righteous—whether it be in our home life, or working life, or ecclesial life—it will be in the measure in which we are holy. Holiness in its noblest sense is a condition where a man is truth-governed and love-mastered; not free from conflict with temptation by any means, but free from the necessity of defeat. Holiness is that inward condition of character built up as a result of fellowship with God.

Holiness, then, is a right relationship towards God revealing itself step by step in a participation of God's character; the development and the outworking in men of submission to the divine will. That is holiness. Its significant feature is that it is inward and has its roots deep in the soul. You will not read it on a man's sleeve, but sometimes it might show on his face.

Now "worship" and "holiness", these two great ideas from 1 Chronicles 16, are linked together by this strange word "beauty": "Worship the Lord in the *beauty* of holiness." The essential thought of the passage gives us a clue to the meaning of beauty. It is not an external decoration, but more of an inherent quality. When a lady puts on her best hat and her prettiest dress, that is a kind of beauty, but it is not the beauty which is meant here: not decoration, but the outshining of some inner character which makes sackcloth look beautiful. Think of the transfiguration of Jesus: that was not the shining upon him of a light from heaven, but rather the shining out from himself of the glory of his perfection, so that even his raiment became white and glistening—not of itself, but because of that which was within it.

"Beauty"

Now this is the essential nature of the beauty of God. We speak of God's love, God's majesty and God's glory, but not often of God's beauty—yet everything which is of God is essentially beautiful. Nothing which has come from God is ugly or repulsive. If any of the created things are such, they have come to that condition as a result of the hand of man. Trees are not ugly, except when some man has tried to cut them or spoil their shape. The beauty of God shines on every blade of grass and every tree and every bird.

When Jesus compared Solomon with the flowers on the hillside at Galilee, he was comparing the beauty of Solomon with the beauty of God. The Bible says that the created things declare the glory of God, and giving glory to God is an essential feature of true worship. There is a sense, therefore, in which the created things worship God by their beauty. And how do they worship? By being true to the law which God has implanted in them. They worship God in the uprising of their blossom, and fruit, and form. They are what God intended them to be, and being that, they give Him glory and He is worshipped in them.

And so by these illustrations we come to man. When does a man worship? When he is what God intended him to be. God does not expect a tulip to do an eagle's work, nor does He expect to gather figs from the apple tree. What God expects of man is a reflection of Himself. Hear the word of Genesis: "Let us make man in our image ...". An approximation to the character of God in humanity: that is manhood—what God intended humanity to be.

And this we have seen in Christ: "The Word was made flesh, and dwelt among us, and we beheld his glory ... *full* of grace and truth." That is beauty, and that is manhood. When the word of God is upon a man and he answers that, and in the uprising of his life he develops his character into the form and beauty of the manhood of Jesus—that is worship. When the Old Testament says that there is no beauty in him that we should desire him (Isaiah 53:2), do not think it means that he was not beautiful. It means that though the beauty was there, we were too dull and too blinded to see it. Isaiah says: “He that shutteth his eyes from seeing evil ... he shall see the king in his beauty”.

Notice, then, what worship really is: a life of holiness unfolding the beauty which glorifies God; taking our life and putting it into such relationship to God that it becomes what He intends it should be; discovering His law, answering His law, walking in the way of His appointing, so yielding our life to His purpose.

Observe the solemn lesson that can be learned from this truth. It is possible to exhort and never worship. It is possible to teach a Sunday School class, and never worship; or to sing with all one’s strength, and never worship. The word and the anthem may not rise any higher than the ceiling of the house—unless the singer’s life yesterday and tomorrow is found in His law and answering His word, responsive to His command.

But coming here today in this act of symbolic worship, in breaking bread in memory of our Saviour, we can remind ourselves once again of the perpetual and unending truth: that life lived within His will must be a life of holiness, for that is the beauty that glorifies God. So we may join with David, with the angels and with all nature, and “worship the LORD in the beauty of holiness”.

4

JOASH—PIETY ON CRUTCHES
(2 CHRONICLES 24)

START by thinking of Athaliah who was married to Jehoram. Together they were a daredevil pair. Their youngest son Ahaziah was made king of Judah and he proved to be as wicked as his parents. He lasted only one year, but it was a year of idolatry and evil. As soon as Ahaziah died his mother Athaliah, with fiendish cruelty, destroyed all the royal children so that she could grasp the reins of power over the house of Judah. I said *all* the royal children, but as you know there was one who escaped. That one was Joash, young baby son of Ahaziah. Little Joash had a wicked grandmother, but he had a good auntie. Her name was Jehosheba, sister of Ahaziah. She was the wife of the high priest—Jehoiada. When Athaliah was slaying the royal children, Jehosheba hid little Joash and he was brought up in secret in his auntie's house. Consequently he was under the care and guidance of his uncle Jehoiada the priest.

Crowned King of Judah

When Joash was seven years old they brought him forth and proclaimed him the rightful king of Judah. They crowned him in the temple and his wicked grandmother Athaliah was executed. This young boy came to be the king of Judah in the line of David. Because of his tender years, his uncle carefully directed his counsels, and instructed him in the principles of good living and good government. And young Joash as he developed, proved to be a good ruler; he did that which was right in the sight of the Lord. He had a great zeal for the house of God. The slackness of the priests was something which troubled him and he made it one of his duties to stir them up. He held the holy scripture in great esteem.

> "And he (Jehoiada) brought forth the king's son, and put the crown upon him, and gave him the testimony; and they made him king, and anointed him; and they clapped their hands, and said, God save the King." (2 Kings 11:12)

So they gave him a copy of the law as they gave Queen Elizabeth II a copy of the Bible at her coronation. Joash loved it and kept it.

A Man of Piety and Wisdom

He was not a man who kept his religion just for the Sabbath day. He put his religion into every day—into the business of life and into the business of the state. I say deliberately "the state", because Joash would not allow sweating and grinding in government departments. If you read on in 2 Chronicles 24 you find that in the work of repairing the temple every tradesman was treated faithfully. Carpenters and masons and other tradesmen all had proper wages. I suppose it would be true to say that Joash was the first real trade union leader! He certainly secured for each man the best possible conditions. Under his supervision the house of God was repaired after the ravages made upon it. Eventually there was continual worship in the house of God and joy in the hearts of the people—though it must be admitted that some of the people still worshipped in the high places instead of the temple.

So this young Joash, under the guidance of his uncle, proved to be upright in character, straight in conduct and religious in spirit. It must have rejoiced the heart of Jehoiada to see the young king's piety and wisdom. Recall how the record tells us about it:

> "And Joash did that which was right in the sight of the LORD all the days of Jehoiada the priest."
>
> (2 Chronicles 24:2)

It is a fine commendation.

Subsequent Failure

But in the Bible every word is important and there is a strong hint here of trouble to come. There is a wealth of significance in the words "all the days of Jehoiada the priest". To realize it we need to read 2 Chronicles 24:22:

> "Joash the king remembered not the kindness which Jehoiada his father had done to him, but slew his son."

What a remarkable thing. This good man turned from God and slew the son of his best friend and wise counsellor. From being earnestly religious, this man suddenly became degenerate and profligate, and when the son of his uncle tried to save him he ordered him to be stoned to death. Would anybody have believed that so much wickedness lay hidden in the heart of a man so circumspect and devout? Is there any explanation for this change—for this abject failure? There usually is a reason when something like this happens. David is an example—the man after God's own heart doing what he did with Bathsheba. When you analyse it the reasons emerge. What is the explanation in the case of Joash? It is this: there was an unseen factor in his character.

Goodness on Crutches

Joash was one of those people who have no root in themselves. He had goodness but it depended for its existence upon circumstances outside himself. So long as Joash was under the guidance and control of his uncle Jehoiada he was a good man. But it was goodness on crutches. When his uncle died Joash went to pieces. There are some people who become like the company they keep—whichever way it is. When they are with the good, they are good. When they are with the bad, they forget their goodness. So it was with Joash. He had no root in himself. He was alright whilst he was on leading reins. He leaned upon others in goodness and in wickedness. Instead of mastering circumstances, he was mastered by them. He lacked independence, courage, strength. To quote the word of the King—he had no salt in himself.

Think of the seed which fell on the stony ground. Stony ground sometimes means soil in which there are a lot of loose stones—but that is not its meaning in the parable. Stony ground here is a thin layer of soil on a bed of rock. Shallow soil is like a superficial character: Joash was one like this. There was no depth in him—what he did was on the surface. The seed sprang up quickly, the parable says, and then withered away quickly because it had no depth of root.

Joash was enthusiastic about wages and conditions. He was keen about repairs and renewals. He responded heartily to the idea of married life. He married not one wife, but two—right away! But you'll notice they were chosen by his uncle. He was probably a man quickly and easily moved; susceptible to every thought and every feeling; his responses were vehement. In the parable it says of those likened to stony ground: "they received the word with joy". So long as the sun shines so does the loyalty. So long as there is happiness the generous emotions expand. But when the circumstances change so does the spirit.

The parable says, "because they had no root they withered away". Now this is the story of Joash. Notice that the shallow soil had beneath it a hard bed of rock, and it is not without significance that often slightness and inconstancy are found together with hardness and violence. It was tragically true in the case of Joash. He was a man of amenable nature—pliable and responsive to the best influences. Then suddenly he is revealed as a man whose heart is as hard as a nether millstone; ready and glad to forget all the blessed advice given by his uncle; ready and glad to cast aside all the wise influences of the formative years; keen to shed the leading strings only to be fettered by his own corrupt desires and his own violent nature.

A Sad Life

What a sad life—that which began best, ended worst. After many years of faithfulness he played the traitor. The worship of Baal and Ashteroth was revived and he ordered murder in the court of the Lord's house. He is mentioned in the New Testament inferentially, in Matthew 23:35—the words of Christ to the Pharisees:

> "That upon you may come all the righteous blood shed upon the earth, from the blood of the righteous Abel unto the blood of Zacharias son of Barachias, whom ye slew between the temple and the altar."

It means that those Pharisees were of the same confederacy of evil as Joash. The reference therefore to this man is a reference of infamy.

After a 40-year reign Joash died in his bed, and although he was in his bed because of illness, he died violently, by the hand of two of his servants, and he was buried—but not in the sepulchres of the kings.

Lessons to be Learned

It is a sad and gloomy story and the only good for us is that we might be able to learn a lesson. Let us notice first of all what the lesson is not. It is not that we ought to despise the guidance and instruction of others. Some men despise those who are in leading strings but we ought not to be ashamed of leading strings. The influence of a godly home is of great value. There is not much grit in a man if he is willing to hear his home ridiculed without protest. It is no mark of manliness to be ashamed of godly parentage. It is better to have a praying washerwoman for a mother than a painted doll. So never despise the guidance, care and instruction of others. But we must remember this. God does not keep his man in cotton wool all the time. Good homes have to be left, and holy relatives and pious friends pass away. Temptation has to be faced and sometimes the devil is an angel of light. God takes away the props so that we may get strength to stand up and be counted. Jesus said we must have salt in ourselves. We cannot live for ever on other people's goodness. Sometimes there are people who take their opinions second hand—they adopt a certain way of life because others are in it. They do things because others whom they respect do them. But in the end it is not the best reason. The faith that is in you must be your own faith. God's grace for one man is not sufficient for two. You must at last get the real thing in your soul. You must know that the Truth is true for yourself.

And the reason is this: what you actually do for Christ will depend upon what you really believe about him. How passionately you believe in him and his cause will determine how passionately you work for his Kingdom. It is vital, because sooner or later you will come to the test as Joash did. There are those who love the Truth while the Truth is nice and the sun is bright. But when the sun is darkened and the landscape is shadowed and happiness is turned to hardness, then they tend to fall away. They are like those in the parable who received the word with joy but when tribulation or persecution arose because of the word, they were offended. The parable gives us the explanation: they had no root in themselves. When the life of discipleship is lived out faithfully it is never easy. By its very nature it tests our character.

Evading Responsibilities

To some extent it is possible to delay the tests by avoiding the issues. You can live in such a way that the difficulties are evaded and the responsibilities are sidestepped and shed. We hear the voice which says to us every day: "Spare thyself—this shall not be unto thee". "Spare thyself, spare thyself"—it is a voice at last which leads to milk and water discipleship; a pale imitation of what Christ meant by "Follow me".

So the lesson is pre-eminently to have salt in yourselves; to get the real Truth and hold it fast; to believe it with all your heart and act in accordance with it. When the test comes, hold fast to it and do not tone it down and explain it away. Stand up and be counted. What is needed is determination not dilution. Be devoted not dilettante. The supreme example is the one who set his face steadfastly to go to Jerusalem, and never flinched. He did not, as other men have done, adroitly wind his way through life avoiding the dangerous forms of evil, sidestepping the issues of life and dodging the difficulties. It is possible through compromise to escape his reproach. He was never like that. Because he was good and just and true he awakened against himself the rage of impurity and injustice and falsehood. He came to stand at last alone at the place of his execution because of his fidelity to the Truth.

Let us finish on a positive note. Christ is our saviour and he is the same yesterday, today and for ever. Let us put our trust in him and believe what he has promised. Whom God makes to stand nothing can overthrow. In this age of hustle and bustle and sensationalism, never forget that the Truth stands firm and the Truth stands fast. You can depend upon it—in the end it will be vindicated and verified. The harvest of a true and faithful life cannot fail. Life is *being*, not *having*. In the end it is what a man is, not what he has that will count. What we have will perish; what we are will abide. So let us seek to be faithful, loyal, and true unto the end. Let us make sure our roots are set firmly in the things that are at the centre of our faith, leaning on none other than the Redeemer himself. I commend to you those words in Colossians 1:

> "And you … hath he reconciled in the body of his flesh through death, to present you holy and unblameable and unreproveable in his sight: if ye continue in the faith grounded and settled, and be not moved away from the hope of the gospel, which ye have heard." (verses 21–23)

It is that we have come to celebrate. Let us do it reverently, declaring our faith in the Lord Jesus Christ, crucified, risen, triumphant and soon to come in glory.

5

"BLESSED IS HE ... WHOSE SIN IS COVERED" (PSALM 32)

THERE are some things in Psalm 32 which if they are looked at superficially are difficult to understand. It is one of those psalms which needs to be read carefully several times in order to grasp the real significance of its teaching. When this is done one of the first things to become evident is that this man is not theorising, but speaking out of the sorrow and the joy of his own deep experience.

It is a song which sobs with sorrow and exults with joy. Underlying the figure which the singer uses there are deep feelings of bitterness and disappointment, of despair and loneliness. That is why its teaching is so valuable to those who share the same common human experiences. He has passed through the valley and through the great darkness, and come at last into the light. He has stood in the presence of the great silence, but hears at last the voice of assurance, and of counsel. He has been overwhelmed with sorrow but at last he has received succour.

Take the very first stanza, the first verse:

> "Blessed *is he whose* transgression is forgiven, *whose* sin is covered."

That is not really what this man said in the Hebrew. Look at verse 1 again, and miss out the words in italics, which have been added by the translators. You will notice, for instance, that there is no personal pronoun "he". The singer is not speaking of some other man or some composite man. What he said was this: "O the blessing of transgression forgiven and sin covered!" He is describing something which God has done for him when he was in the depth of despair and sorrow and silence. It is a doxology—a great expression of praise to God for the deliverance which has come to the sorrowing man.

At the end of the song, there is the same note of praise:

> "Be glad in the LORD, and rejoice, ye righteous: and shout for joy, all ye that are upright in heart." (verse 11)

And in between the opening praise and the ending praise he tells of his feelings and his experiences, when there was no light upon the pathway and great chillness in his soul; and why he is constrained to sing out, "O the blessing of transgression forgiven and sin covered!"

He speaks of "sin" and "transgression" and "iniquity". These are all different aspects of failure. Behind the word "transgression" is the idea of a conscious breaking of the law—a deliberate setting aside of a commandment. Underlying the word "sin" is the idea of missing the mark, of seeking to rise up to a standard but falling miserably short. It may be that your experience has never taken you into the realms of transgression, but I feel sure it will have taken you into the realm of sin. The word "iniquity" conveys the idea of not so much the thing done but the state of sinfulness which arises from the sin.

"In whose spirit there is no guile"

The psalmist knew the desolating power of all these aspects of sin. He knew the dark, despairing degradation that settles on a man's mind when he is convicted of his own wickedness; the loneliness which hangs like an icicle upon a man's heart and makes him feel severed from all others and from God. So the psalmist turns from his doxology to state the truth in relation to the individual soul:

> "Blessed is the man unto whom the LORD imputeth not iniquity, and in whose spirit there is no guile." (verse 2)

We ought to be very glad that he did not say, 'Blessed is the man to whom his neighbour imputeth not iniquity'. Has your experience taught you that it is a more blessed thing to be judged by God than by men; that it is easier to please God than to please men? The psalmist had learned it. He had discovered that God is more reasonable, more patient and more just than men.

Perhaps one of the most wonderful things about the Kingdom of God is going to be that the King shall not judge by the sight of his eyes or the hearing of his ears, but his judgements are to be righteous. That is to say, they will be based upon a perfect knowledge of all the underlying facts and all the invisible issues. So it is with God and sin and forgiveness. Underneath the eyes of fire there is the voice of love. The judge will acquit the guilty altogether—he will not impute any iniquity. The transgression is forgiven; the sin is covered.

But there is a condition. It is something in the man "in whose spirit there is no guile". If guile is cast out by the man, God will cast out the sin. What is guile? Guile means 'seeking to hide', 'to deceive', 'to cloak over'. On the face of it, it may sound ridiculous to say that we can hide anything from God, that we can really deceive Him. We may say that no man can practise guile in the presence of God. But let us not be too sure—David did!

How often do *we* argue in our minds and therefore in God's presence that some evil thing is not so very evil? How often do we seek to make plausible the wrong things in our lives which we know we ought to shed but which we want to keep? How often do we give mean things exalted names to try to make them more acceptable? Or how often do we try to have one room in our house which is marked 'private', where only we may go; or one half-hour in the day when God must be excluded? Or how often do we just refuse to face the truth about ourselves? This is guile; this is deceit; this is seeking to hide the real position. And where there is guile, God imputes iniquity.

But if there be no cloaking and no hiding and no plausible arguing; if a man says, 'I will excuse this thing no longer, it has been hidden long enough, it is wrong and I have sinned—God be merciful'; then in a moment, swift as lightning and swifter, gentle as the first breaking of the sunlight, God pronounces on that man the verdict of the guiltless. He is acquitted. He is free, and in his relief sings out: "O the blessing of transgression forgiven and sin covered!"

But there is a contrary experience—and the psalmist dwells on it. It is the experience of the man who knows he ought not to practise guile in the presence of the Lord, but does; who knows he ought to come out into the light, but is hidden away—cloaking the evil, hiding the sin. So this man had the same experience and tells his feelings:

> "When I kept silence, my bones waxed old through my roaring all the day long. For day and night thy hand was heavy upon me: my moisture is turned into the drought of summer." (verses 3,4)

He is saying: 'I put a bold face on it; in my bravado I tried to convince myself that God did not care—but there was no peace and no life.' This reminds us of Peter, warming himself by the world's fire, but keeping in his heart a coldness that no fire would ever warm.

Notice the figure he uses: "My moisture was dried up as in the drought of summer." This is the picture of a tree withering from dryness, dying for lack of moisture. In Psalm 104:16 you will read this: "The trees of the LORD are full ...". The translators have added the words "of sap". That is a great pity. Prosaically they thought that trees are only full of sap. But that word "sap" covers a great deal. It means life and beauty and fulfilment. It is like a man when he is right with God: his life is full and free and high. He is fulfilling his destiny; he is manhood at its truest and noblest. He is like a tree full of sap. But the man with sin hidden and unconfessed is like a tree dried up, half dead, withered—appearing respectable outside but inwardly soured and fevered, with no rest and no joy.

And this condition the psalmist traces to the very activity of God: "Day and night thy hand was heavy upon me" (Psalm 32:4). This may sound severe, but it is the love of God in action. The man means that when he wanted to forget the reality of his sin, the Lord kept alive the consciousness of his iniquity. When we think the matter is concluded God sustains the controversy in our hearts. The sin, the habit, the enticement which we know is wrong, but which we will not confess—how it haunts us! God gives His children no rest when their waywardness brings them into jeopardy. He places obstacles in the path to halt their wilfulness: "Thy hand was heavy upon me." He will not let us escape to destruction. It is love which chastens us.

Whilst this thought is in our minds, notice verses 8 and 9. By the strange processes of inspiration the psalmist speaks the words of God Himself:

> "I will instruct thee and teach thee in the way which thou shalt go: I will counsel thee ... Be ye not as the horse, or as the mule, which have no understanding: whose trappings must be bit and bridle to hold them in, else they will not come near unto thee" (RV).

Notice then in the context of God's overriding care and guidance of His children, two ways which a man may go: by understanding—that is, by an inward impelling motive which understands what the will of the Lord is, and finds delight in doing it; and by bit and bridle—which is by a compelling pressure from outside, from circumstances which curb, hurt, check, master, so that the powers of a man's life may be realised at last, even through chastening. Jesus is the finest example of the first: "I delight to do thy will, O my God." Most of us to a greater or lesser degree are or have been examples of the second. Let us not think that the use of bit and bridle means the elimination of our will. If any man tells you that a mule whom you are seeking to control by bit and bridle has no will—then you can be sure he has never met a mule. But in the processes of God's chastening, the weaker will can be mastered by the stronger.

But observe in verse 5 what the man tells us about the things which happened when he acknowledged his sin: "I said, I will confess my transgressions unto the LORD; and thou forgavest the iniquity of my sin." It seems that the great God did not even wait for the actual confession to be made, but in the very moment the man *resolved* to confess, the Lord met him. This is a true picture of God the Father.

"I will confess my transgressions"

Recall the story of the wandering boy who left home and came to deep degradation; and then when he came to himself, resolved to return home and seek reinstatement as a servant in his father's house. The father was looking out every day to see if his boy was coming home. And one day he saw him a great way off—and the father did not wait for him to come in and plead for forgiveness. While the lad was a great way off, the father ran out and fell on his neck and kissed him. That is a true picture of God. Any child of God, out in the world, degraded by sin, burdened by transgression, cold with loneliness: if such a one at this very moment will say, "I will confess my sin, I will arise and go to my Father and say, Father, I have sinned against heaven and before thee"—in that very moment of decision, God will forgive. God does not wait for formalities, for the Sabbath day, for the last hour of evening. He waits only for that moment when the heart casts aside its guile and turns to Him.

This then explains the feelings which underlie the expression of relief at the beginning: "O the blessing of transgression forgiven and sin covered!" So when a man is guileless before God his sin is dealt with, and he is delivered from sorrow:

> "Surely when the great waters overflow they shall not reach unto him. Thou art my hiding place; thou wilt preserve me from trouble; thou wilt compass me about with songs of deliverance." (verses 6,7, RV)

It does not mean that there is a promise of freedom from sorrow or trouble. But it does mean that the sorrow will not master him; that the trouble will not overwhelm him.

It's true, isn't it? Great waters have gone over us, but we are not destroyed. In the midst of trouble we have found a hiding place. Nearer to us than all the harm of circumstances is the care of God. We have listened to the whisper of His word, and have taken courage. We have yielded to the constraint of His guidance, and are preserved.

Coming now to the table of remembrance, we have even more cause than David to feel the blessing of forgiveness. What David foresaw in faith, we know as certainty—“that God was in Christ, reconciling the world unto himself, not imputing their trespasses unto them” (2 Corinthians 5:19).

6

TRUST IN THE LORD (PSALM 118)

READING Psalm 118 it is evident that one of the important issues which it emphasises is the need to trust in God. Remember verses 8 and 9:

> "It is better to trust in the LORD than to put confidence in man. It is better to trust in the LORD than to put confidence in princes."

It provokes us to have confidence in the promises that have been made and given to us by the Lord God Almighty: "The LORD is on my side; I will not fear: what can man do unto me?" (verse 6). You will recall that this very verse is quoted in Hebrews: "So that we may boldly say, The Lord is my helper, and I will not fear what man shall do unto me" (13:6). That little phrase, "we may boldly say", is a declaration of confidence. People who are confident can be bold, and this confidence is rooted in trust.

Trust in Everyday Life

Have you ever thought that at all levels of life it is trust which makes living possible? Life without trust would be a nightmare. Trust is the very foundation of almost everything we do. At the start of the day, when we run to catch the train or the bus, we have to trust that the driver knows the way and will stop at the right places. At work we have to trust in the judgements made by our colleagues; we have to trust the safety procedures provided for our protection. When it comes to lunchtime we have to trust that what is set before us has been prepared to help us and not to harm us. We have to trust that the chef is a friend and not a poisoner; we eat in trust. If we had to check a meal for malice before we could eat it our lives would be intolerable. The whole world of business holds together on a great system of trust. Men trade and give credit on trust. You keep your money in the bank because you trust it will be safe. Those in school or college have to trust their teachers. We have to accept knowledge that we have no opportunity to prove—we accept it on trust.

When it comes to the most intimate of relationships, trust is paramount. Homes are homely because of trust. Jealousy and suspicion make them places of torment. Friendship is based on trust. If your brother cannot trust you, how can you be his friend? The point I am striving to make is that since trust is at the very centre of ordinary life, it is ten times more true about religious life. It is trust which turns conviction into faith. Trust is faith in action. This is what Psalm 118 is telling us—whatever happens we must trust in God. Abraham had to trust God when he left home to go to a land he did not know and which he had never seen. Noah had to trust God when he was told to build a very big vessel in the middle of dry land. Moses gave up his status as an Egyptian prince to become an outcast with the people of God, because he trusted the word of the Lord. Hannah left her burden with the Lord because she trusted Him. Asa fought against tremendous odds because he trusted in the God of battles. The woman with the issue of blood touched tremblingly the hem of the Lord's garment because somehow she trusted the man from Nazareth. Paul was able to say he will present you holy, unblameable and unreproveable because he could trust in the One who makes it possible. And the man of the seamless robe was able to face the cross-crowned hill because he trusted in his God and his Father. No wonder the psalmist tells us that it is better to trust in the Lord than put confidence in man.

Knowledge of God

Here is something to ponder: why did all these people put their trust in God? What is the ground for trust? Well, hear the word of the psalmist again: "They that know thy name will put their trust in thee" (Psalm 9:10). So the reason for trust is what we know of God. The warrant of faith is the divine character. There was a time in the life of King David when his enemies assaulted his faith. They said unto him, "Where is thy God?" They meant 'He is impotent, He never does anything; what good is He to you?' David was worried and disquieted by this and you will remember he speaks about it in Psalm 42: "Why art thou cast down, O my soul? And why art thou disquieted in me?" (verse 5). And then in his distress he falls back on his knowledge of God. He says, 'I remember how He dealt with me at Jordan and Hermon and Mizar, how He succoured me and saved me. He commanded His loving kindness in the daytime and in the night His song was with me'.

So that is the secret of trust—your *knowledge* of God. And it is especially true when you are venturing on an unknown way; when you are stepping out into new circumstances or facing some unaccustomed experience. There are so many unknowns on the journey of life. How shall we make any progress? Well, trust in God; measure the problem of the unknown way by the problem of the trackless wilderness, for He who led then will lead again. The world before us is strong and hostile: how shall we overcome? Well, trust in God; He who was able to save in Egypt is able to save in Canaan. "They that know thy name will put their trust in thee" (Psalm 9:10). It is incontrovertible—trust is fixed in what you know of God and in your experience of His power and love. Jesus once said to Jairus when news came that his daughter was dead, "Fear not: believe only".

"I will never leave thee ..."

Because God is righteous He cannot do wrong. Because God is love He can only act lovingly. Unbelief will try to deny this, as it did in David's day. But have none of it. In spite of the mystery, in spite of the anguish, in spite of the trial, notwithstanding the uncertainty, the adversity, the hostility—put your trust in the Lord. He has said, "I will never leave thee, nor forsake thee". If that is not true, then prophets, apostles and the Messiah have all deceived us. Abraham was sure of the unknown land because he was utterly sure of the unseen God. This principle is timeless: "whom having not seen, we love" (1 Peter 1:8). Our trust is not in pundits or princes, parliaments or policies, else we should be of all men most pitiable. Nor is it in circumstances, else we should be at the mercy of every passing change. Our trust is in the living God.

I know you may be thinking it is easy to say that, but more difficult to live in accordance with it. I know that—like you I have natural fears. But that is the purpose of this moment of memorial. It is designed to fortify our faith, to give us blessed assurance once more in this one great redeeming act of atonement; that through the bruising to death of this one man, our salvation is assured, and we can be forgiven and made new.

So in this solemn moment of bread breaking let us say: "Father in heaven, we trust you and our confidence is in your Son, the beloved, and in his redeeming blood." May we each feel it to be true.

7

THE SECRET OF HAPPINESS
(PROVERBS 3)

THINK for a moment of two passages—one in the Old Testament, and one in the New Testament. We will take them in that order—Old Testament first:

"In all thy ways acknowledge him, and he shall direct thy paths." (Proverbs 3:6)

Think of the word "acknowledge". The idea at the root of it is that of vision. It means in all ways see God. It calls on us to recognise the activity of God in every part of our life. It means believe in Him, pray to Him, fear Him—but more than this—recognise that He has authority over everything that we do. The word says: "in all thy ways". It means what it says. Let the principles of God's revelation be applied to every activity. Take account of His teaching in every decision you make. Do nothing without learning about God's will, as it is revealed in His word. In other words let your religion be seen in every department of life—home life, family life, work and career, recreation and pleasure.

Just take one example because it is the most unlikely—recreation. Acknowledging Him means to have no recreation which dulls your perception of God, or diminishes your respect for His word, or encourages you to neglect His service, or be careless about your brother in Christ. See God in the dark as well as in the light. And the promise is that "He shall direct thy paths". When that happens, the likelihood of happiness is at its highest. Could there be a better life than the life directed by our Heavenly Father? He has many strange ways of directing. He directs by opening doors or by shutting doors. He directs by disappointment or by encouragement. He directs by a deeper vision of the meaning of His revealed word. But it means you will be where He wants you to be and you will be doing what He wants you to do. Although it will not necessarily be roses all the way measured by human standards, it will bring joy and peace, and these are God's words for happiness.

Now to the New Testament passage:

> "I have learned, in whatsoever state I am, therewith to be content. I know both how to be abased, and I know how to abound: every where and in all things I am instructed both to be full and to be hungry, both to abound and to suffer need. I can do all things through Christ which strengtheneth me." (Philippians 4:11–13)

"I have learned in whatsoever state I am, therewith to be content": that is the secret of happiness. If Paul was in want or if he was in abundance, in either state he was content. How was it achieved? Well, think of what the possibilities are. First of all the monastic method: shut yourself away and remove the chance of being in either condition. That is detachment by separation. Next the Stoic's method: whether in want or in plenty, steel yourself against it—just try to endure it—following the old dictum, 'that which cannot be cured will have to be endured'. Adopt a hard, flinty spirit set to suffer the effects of want or plenty. This might be described as detachment by opposition.

Then the method of the Apostle Paul: that is, whether in conditions of want or conditions of plenty, make use of the circumstances and get the best out of them. If in want, do not be dismayed and if in plenty, do not be worried and guilty. Accept that either condition has opportunities for something good to be done or achieved. The realisation must be that in want or in plenty Christ is present and Christ is aware of the situation, and—according to Paul—Christ will strengthen those who put their trust in him. So the secret of Paul in this situation is detachment by use. Use either condition to the best advantage.

Now if you are able to see life in this way, that is by faith to be detached either way from abundance or need—not allowing these things to affect you in the wrong way, but "therewith to be content"—then this is the road to happiness. To quote the words of 1 Timothy 6:6: "Godliness with contentment is great gain". If you are poor make the most of what you have; if you are rich make sure you use your riches to make others who are poor more comfortable. In this way both are helped. It is like manna: those who gathered little and those who gathered much were both filled. This is joy.

The wise man could see the dangers inherent in either extreme and prayed that he might be spared them:

> "Give me neither poverty nor riches; feed me with food convenient for me: lest I be full, and deny thee, and say,

> Who is the LORD? Or lest I be poor, and steal, and take the name of my God in vain." (Proverbs 30:8,9)

But if these things are to be the means of our proving, then let us be exhorted by the writer to the Hebrews:

> "Let your conversation (*manner of life*) be without covetousness; and be content with such things as ye have: for he hath said, I will never leave thee, nor forsake thee. So that we may boldly say, The Lord is my helper, and I will not fear what man shall do unto me."
> (Hebrews 13:5,6)

8

THE BLESSINGS OF THE KINGDOM (ISAIAH 40)

IN order to help me with this little exhortation, I have to ask for your co-operation—that is to try to go back in your minds to about 1900 and just after. I realise that it cannot be an actual remembrance of the time, but a recollection of what you have been told and the evidence you have seen or read. Think of those times then—they were times of plenty in some ways and times of shortages in other ways. There was plenty of destitution; there was a shortage of affluence. They were hard times. There was no dole; there were no pensions; if you were out of work you were destitute. The ecclesia in Oxford used to pay a brother sixpence per week to light and dowse the candles in our meeting room—well, it helped to feed his children. They bought a second-hand mangle for a widow so that she could take in washing and keep the wolf from the door. Scarlet fever was then a notifiable disease and a sister's children caught it, and the father could not go to work for seven weeks—he had to be isolated because of the fever. No work, no money. The day came when the sister had to say to the baker: "This is my last copper, do not call again I have nothing to pay with". The baker was a good man. He said, "Whilst I have bread you will have bread". They were hard times. Sometimes there were buttons in the collection bag. The recording brother, commenting somewhat wryly upon that, wrote in his record: "it is hoped that this practice will not become regular". But you see, when people have only buttons to give they are very poor. Yes—they were hard times.

Visions of the Kingdom

Here is the thing to realise. Into that hard world there came a shaft of joy; there came the Gospel of the Kingdom of God. Beset by the hardness of life it was a source of master comfort. It was sweetness being poured into the rancid stream of life. It was a little saffron being cast upon the dullness of the day. It was light into darkness, a song in the night. It promised joy for sadness; sorrow was succoured and there was healing for their wounds. They loved it and loved to hear about it. The idea of postponing the coming of the

Kingdom was the supreme contradiction. It was the one thing they longed for because it answered their need superlatively. The words of the prophets contained many of the passages which they loved so much, and which sustained them in the harsh world in which they lived and by which they were surrounded. Think of these words of Isaiah:

"Behold, a king shall reign in righteousness, and princes shall rule in judgment. And a man shall be as an hiding place from the wind, and a covert from the tempest; as rivers of water in a dry place, as the shadow of a great rock in a weary land. And the eyes of them that see shall not be dim, and the ears of them that hear shall hearken." (Isaiah 32:1–3)

"Behold, the Lord GOD will come with strong hand, and his arm shall rule for him: behold, his reward is with him, and his work before him. He shall feed his flock like a shepherd: he shall gather the lambs with his arm, and carry them in his bosom, and shall gently lead those that are with young." (Isaiah 40:10,11)

"Hast thou not known? Hast thou not heard, that the everlasting God, the LORD, the Creator of the ends of the earth, fainteth not, neither is weary? There is no searching of his understanding. He giveth power to the faint; and to them that have no might he increaseth strength. Even the youths shall faint and be weary, and the young men shall utterly fall: but they that wait upon the LORD shall renew their strength; they shall mount up with wings as eagles; they shall run, and not be weary; and they shall walk, and not faint." (Isaiah 40:28–31)

"I will open rivers in high places, and fountains in the midst of the valleys: I will make the wilderness a pool of water, and the dry land springs of water." (Isaiah 41:18)

"Behold my servant, whom I uphold; mine elect, in whom my soul delighteth ... he shall not cry, nor lift up, nor cause his voice to be heard in the street. A bruised reed shall he not break, and the smoking flax shall he not quench: he shall bring forth judgment unto truth." (Isaiah 42:1–3)

"I will pour water upon him that is thirsty, and floods upon the dry ground: I will pour my spirit upon thy seed, and my blessing upon thine offspring." (Isaiah 44:3)

People were moved deeply by the wooing winsomeness of the word of God. Many a weary head has rested upon those words of comfort. Many a broken spirit has found healing and hope in those sentences. Many a fearful and frightened soul has taken courage from those promises. These words have a profound effect upon the people of God because they are profound words. No wonder in time past they loved the vision so dearly and saw it so clearly. It was the master passion of their faith. What I am doing today, 80–90 years ago they did regularly; that is, dwell longingly upon the blessings of the Kingdom of God.

Old-Fashioned Exhortation

This is an old-fashioned exhortation. Its purpose is not to make you feel bad, or disturbed or embarrassed; but I must tell you that I believe that early enthusiasm about the blessings of the Kingdom has diminished in some quarters. What once thrilled our forefathers, today seems to bore some Christadelphians. Proof—the very poor support at our Sunday evening meetings when the Gospel of the Kingdom is preached. Sometimes the reasons for being absent are unbelievably paltry:

- "We had friends come to tea"
- "We had to help the children with their homework"
- "We arranged a barbecue"
- "We can come only once on Sunday"
- "I have to get ready for Monday"

It is something to ponder and to remember that the things which are at the centre of our faith were once rousing, invigorating and exciting. We must ensure that they still are, and respond to them with the enthusiasm which moved our forebears. There is a tendency today sometimes to tone down the emphasis on what are called the blessings of the Kingdom, but I want to tell you something—not by this preacher. Let us be re-convinced that these things are the things which in our deepest heart we long for and which ought to shine more brightly as the outer darkness intensifies.

The point I want to stress now is that, just as in the days of a century ago when the wonderful words of the Bible about the Kingdom of God made an especial appeal to God's people in the peculiar circumstances of their times, so even today the same principle applies. These are days of fear and insecurity, when hearts are beginning to fail and when people are beset with anxiety about the forces which thrive on violence and terror. These are days when people are afraid almost to move about the streets of the city where they live; where the bomber and the mugger and the forces of impurity are abroad.

Playing in the Streets

Our exhortation dwells on the material blessings of the Kingdom of God—and one in particular. To pursue it I must ask your pardon for being personal and speaking about my own affairs in Oxford for a minute or two. My job is in the Parks and Recreation Department of the City Council and the policy of that department is to get children off the streets into parks and playgrounds. Where children are compelled to play in the streets it is a reproach to our department. This ought not to be and we are committed to see that it does not happen in this city. But here is a thing to ponder. Before long a city is going to be built in which there will be a playground and believe it or not the playground will be in the streets—the children's playground in the city of God:

> Thus saith the LORD of hosts; There shall yet old men and old women dwell in the streets of Jerusalem, and every man with his staff in his hand for very age. And the streets of the city shall be full of boys and girls playing in the streets thereof. (Zechariah 8:4,5)

How you regard that depends upon your outlook. The Road Safety Officer will be shocked; the Recreation Manager will be sad. Some people might say: "Well, that is marvellous". Notice what God says (verse 6):

> "Thus saith the LORD of hosts; If it be marvellous in the eyes of the remnant of this people in these days, should it also be marvellous in mine eyes? saith the LORD of hosts."

This is another way of saying that the thing which surprises you, shocks you and makes you marvel is the very thing upon which the heart of God is set, and which is right there in His city and in the centre of His purpose. Children are going to play, they are going to play together and they are going to play together in the streets.

Those words are symptomatic of the peace and the purity and the power of God's government: the establishment of His kingdom, the building of His city, the healing of all wounds, the realisation of all the forces which make for the perfection of life. Zechariah was a stern prophet who had no soft and easy things to say in the face of the iniquities which abounded in Israel, and which would bring them at last to disgrace and degradation. But in the midst of the thunder he saw the glory of God and heard the music of the ages. Reading the prophecy up to this point you would hardly think that his mind would be concerned with play. And then suddenly, moved by the Holy Spirit, out of his deep heart, illuminated by the vision of the day which will come, he sings into the ears of all men everywhere the most poetic description of the Kingdom of God you can find in the Bible: "The streets of the city shall be full of boys and girls playing in the streets thereof". Somebody told me once that it would not really happen because there would be no streets in the city of God—but I prefer Zechariah.

Here is an interesting thing, that all the Millennial references to children in the Bible are to children at play. "And the sucking child shall play on the hole of the asp, and the weaned child shall put his hand on the cockatrice' den" (Isaiah 11:8). There is a day coming when the lion shall eat straw like the ox and the wolf and the lamb shall lie down together in perfect peace, and the child will be with them at play. I have a kind of notion that it is God's will that children and animals are to play together, that this is what He intended, and the old forces still survive instinctively in children. When we took our children to Dudley Zoo they wanted to climb over the barrier to be with the polar bears. Of course my wife would not hear of it, but could it be a divine instinct which presently will be realised? "A little child shall lead them" is a child at play—let us not whittle it down until we have spoiled it. God's ideal for the child is that he shall be at play and the features of a child at play are joy and merriment, earnestness, pity, protection for the weak, the triumph of good. All the forces which realise the government of God are there in miniature in Zechariah's vision. And notice the words carefully: the boys and girls are not only to play in the streets but they are to play together.

No Segregation of the Sexes.

When I was young segregation was the master policy. There was a Boys' Entrance and a Girls' Entrance—separate playgrounds so that the twain never met, except it be nefariously. Our brethren employed in teaching tell me that in the comprehensive system of education segregation is ended and mixing is the new policy. Whether that means that the new system is more divine than the old I cannot tell, but we can be sure of one thing: in the city of God the boys and girls are to play together. The day is coming when naturally, purely, perfectly they will be together. The strength of developing manhood has the effect of strengthening womanhood, and the refinement of womanhood has the effect of refining manhood.

This is God's plan and God's ideal. Therefore the streets of the city shall be full of boys and girls playing together.

City of God

What shall we say to these things? Mark the contrast between the streets of the world and the streets of the city of God. Our streets today are not fit for children; there are too many forces at work which left to themselves would hurt and harm young life—ideologically and physically. But if you can walk in your imagination along the streets of the city of God you can be assured that the children are safe and secure—no perversions, no pollution, no muggers, no cowardly bombers. The love of children is greater than the love of gain. Why is the vision of children in the city of God so important? Because if the city is safe for children it is safe for everyone; because if the children are able to develop their life as God intended then so is everyone. Men are to be refashioned at the very centre of their spiritual life. "They shall not hurt nor destroy in all my holy mountain, saith the LORD."

So finally let us think of two things. Isaiah's words will be realised for certain because all the forces which are against have been mastered by the Messiah. Think of this in John 11:50: "… it is expedient for us, that one man should die for the people, and that the whole nation perish not". John informs us that this is prophetic of Jesus dying for the nation, "and not for that nation only, but that also he should gather together in one the children of God that were scattered abroad" (verse 52). This we have come to celebrate.

And the words of exhortation? In readiness for the day of Isaiah's vision, set up the spirit of the Millennium in your own home, in your life, in your own soul. For if you will realise it at last in the Kingdom of God, you must first realise it today—in all the things which call for peace and purity and power. Crown Christ anew your lawful king, not just theoretically and sentimentally, but by seeking to realise his ideal in your daily life, as Master, Lord and King.

9

THE POTTER AND THE CLAY (JEREMIAH 18)

COME with me to Jeremiah 18 where we read the words of the Lord in verse 2: "Arise, and go down to the potter's house, and there I will cause thee to hear my words." And Jeremiah tells us in verse 3, "Then I went down to the potter's house, and, behold, he wrought a work on the wheels." Let us follow Jeremiah for there is a great lesson to be learned at the potter's house. The figure of the potter and the clay is one that is used powerfully in the holy scriptures. Four great Bible writers use it: Isaiah, Jeremiah, Zechariah and the Apostle Paul—all of them men who exerted a great influence upon their generation and were mighty in their service for God. I am well aware that Jeremiah 18 has an interpretation which is national in its application, but I am not concerned with that now. We could no doubt dwell in an interesting way upon God's dealing with Israel and other nations as revealed in the figure of the potter and the clay, but today I want to take the principles—divine principles—which are revealed in this figure and apply them to our individual and personal lives.

A Familiar Scene

The march of time has caused most processes to give way to modern methods, but I understand that the house of the potter today in the lands of the Bible is almost exactly the same as it was when Jeremiah was there. The wheel may be somewhat different today but there has been no real change in the essential things—the potter and the clay. Let us try to imagine what Jeremiah saw when he went down to that potter's house. He saw the potter, the wheel and the clay. The potter is a man—a capable craftsman—intelligent and creative; the wheel is the instrument which the potter uses to bring into existence the thing which he has in mind; and the clay is a material which can be used in such a way as to accomplish whatever the potter has designed in his plan. It is very easy to identify the significance of the figure: God is the Potter, the wheels are the circumstances of life, and the clay is humanity.

The Potter at Work

As we watch the Potter we see He sits at work at the wheel and places His hand upon the clay. He presses the clay against the whirling wheel, now heavily, now ever so gently. The clay begins to form under His fingers. All the time the Potter is giving close and untiring attention to His work. His eye is never lifted from the clay while the wheels are moving. The clay is plastic and as the Potter presses it against the wheel so it conforms to what He desires. In the mind of the Potter there is the vision of a vessel for use and for beauty, and as we watch we can see that the vision in His mind is being translated into a fact in the clay. The clay by itself is useless and unlovely, but when the hands of the Potter bear upon it we begin to see that this base material is full of wonderful possibilities. And yet we realise that whatever beauty, design and usefulness is achieved in the clay, it is the workmanship of the Potter that has achieved it. His foot is in control of the wheel, His hands are on the clay—He is at work.

Simple Lessons

The lessons of the Potter's house are simple. There we see God, the Master Workman, with the thought of creation in His mind. We see all the circumstances of life in those swiftly turning wheels; turning so swiftly sometimes as to make us afraid and perplexed. In the clay we see ourselves—material which will take the impression of the Potter's fingers.

The clay speaks of man's capacity to respond to God. It can be moulded. You never find iron being pressed upon the wheel of the Potter. Clay is the material for transformation. Man is the only created thing in this universe which can respond to God. Other created things will reflect the glory of God—will reveal the mark of the divine upon them—but only man can respond in love. And as we watch the Potter at work on the wheels with the clay, what awful truth strikes us? Surely this: the absolute sovereignty of the Potter over the clay. He can do just as He pleases. He can if He wills throw out the clay or do as He likes with it. The clay cannot complain, the clay cannot resist—it cannot say to the Potter, I want to be this shape or that. In the words of Paul:

> "Nay but, O man, who art thou that repliest against God? Shall the thing formed say to him that formed it, Why hast thou made me thus?" (Romans 9:20)

We hear a great deal today about the rights of man, but the lesson of the Potter's house teaches us about the rights of God.

God's Sovereignty

Standing by itself this idea of the absolute sovereignty of God is tremendous, awful, frightening. When I think of it standing by itself it makes me afraid. Absolute power is an awful thing and as it is expressed in this figure of the Potter it has caused some men to turn away in rebellion against the whole conception of it. That is because men have thought too much about the sovereignty of God without a thought for the character of God. It is true, absolute power can be tyrannical and that makes it awful to conceive—and yet as we stand and watch the Potter at work there dawns upon our consciousness two other things. This Potter is working to a purpose: "Behold, he wrought his work on the wheels" (Jeremiah 18:3, RV). As we watch we see that the purpose of the Potter is to create a thing of beauty—not a purpose of tyranny but a purpose of love. The clay by quiet submission to the thought of the Potter comes to realise the purpose of the craftsman. The clay under His creative hand becomes a thing of beauty. The thought is in the mind of the Potter—it needs the clay to make it real.

Created in Love

That shows a wonderful thing. Man is created so that God can manifest the things which are in the divine mind. Paul says: "We are his workmanship" (Ephesians 2:10). What he really said was, "We are his *poiema*"—we are his 'poem'. What he meant was, 'We are God's work of art' through which He makes manifest the things of beauty which are in His own mind. Peter says the same thing:

> "But ye are a chosen generation, a royal priesthood, an holy nation, a peculiar people; that ye should shew forth the praises of him who hath called you out of darkness into his marvellous light." (1 Peter 2:9)

And then as we watch at the Potter's house the other thing that comes to our mind is the person of the Potter—who He is and what He is like. Absolute power may frighten us, but when we know the person who wields it we shall understand it better. And as we watch the Potter we realise that it is the God of love who works at the wheels.

Every turn He makes, every pressure He brings to bear, every bend of the clay He imposes—all is done with the motive of love. Nothing is done to destroy; all is done to create and recreate. Nothing is done arbitrarily, nothing is done capriciously; everything is done with love as its driving force. I shall not seek to argue this—it would be an insult; you know it yourselves. God is love. Remember He governs the wheels. There surely ought to be some comfort in this for us.

Formed under Pressure

O think of it: if He almost breaks us by the pressure of His hands, it is to make us at the last. If He seems almost to crush us on the whirling wheels, it is to create us in the end. And how often have we felt the pressure of the Potter's hands and have not known from whence that pressure came. We have been puzzled and perplexed; we have felt beaten and downcast. The 'pressure of life' we call it. We have said in our hearts, "Why does this happen? I have tried to be faithful—this is hard to bear". Brethren, the Potter is making something out of the mass of inert, imperfect clay. It is not done by magic, not in a moment by some mechanical readjustment of things so that the imperfect is immediately perfected, but by processes strange and difficult and profound. By teaching, by pain, by discipline, by affliction, by baptisms of fire and suffering, by crushing, by breaking, by making, by mending, by rekindling—God brings the imperfect to perfection.

So feeling the pressure of His hand we are in agony; we are beset with hard trials; the circumstances of life bear severely upon our little world. The Potter is at the whirling wheels and He has control of them. No man is tried above that which he is able to bear—God makes a way of escape. Remember, "We are his workmanship"; we are His property. Poor and worthless and lacking in beauty, but His property—by redemption. We are not our own; we have been bought with a great price.

Unyielding Clay

Let us watch once again in the Potter's house for there is one last lesson to be learned. He is at work on the wheels, the clay is being fashioned, the hands of the Potter are pressed upon it. And then it does not yield. It breaks; it cracks; it will not conform to the mind of the craftsman. And then it comes to us that the absolute sovereignty of the Potter is limited by the will of the clay. The Potter has imposed upon His own sovereignty this limitation. He will not make the clay into a vessel of beauty if it is unyielding to His touch. In all this strange and wonderful process, in which the Potter plays so great a part, there comes a time when the co-operation of the clay is vital. Two things make the vessel of beauty: the skill of the Potter and the yielding of the clay. They are both vital. The terms of discipleship are these:

> "Whosoever will come after me, let him deny himself, and take up his cross, and follow me." (Mark 8:34)

Sometimes the clay is marred in the Potter's hand and the field at the side of the Potter's house is full of the vessels which have been marred. To rebel is to take the clay out of the Potter's hands and to render it waste.

Some have felt that they have been marred—half-formed—and then not come to perfection. The Potter's field is full of the wreckage of lives that might have been made into vessels of beauty, but because they would not yield or only partly yield to the will of the craftsman at the wheels, they have not come to their real purpose in the plan of God. Have you ever felt, my brethren, that in some ways your life has been spoiled? Have you ever felt that it could have been so much better, and yet it was not? The vessel is not true—it is out of perspective—not in every place has the clay yielded to make that symmetry and beauty which is in the mind of the Master Workman.

Another Vessel

Come with me once again to Jeremiah 18:

> "Then I went down to the potter's house, and behold, he wrought a work on the wheels. And the vessel that he made of clay was marred in the hand of the potter: so he made it again another vessel, as seemed good to the potter to make it." (verses 3,4)

O my brethren there is hope for us yet: "He made it again another vessel". Thanks be to God, the vessels which were thought to be flung away, imperfect, marred, unlovely, He takes again and recreates them, if they will but yield to His love. Surely there is comfort for us in this. If we feel abandoned, God has not left us comfortless. He has hope of us yet. He is able "to present us holy and unblameable and unreproveable in his sight"—if only we can believe it. If you feel yourself to be in the potter's field, there is a message for you today. They bought the potter's field with the price of blood. I know the deal was done in strange company but the price was the blood of the Saviour. The Potter Himself has come down to the midst of the wreckage in the person of His beloved child, Jesus, and has gathered up the wreckage and by the price of His own child's life has bought it. Now the wrecks can be remade and restored. By the mystery of God's Son being sold as a slave, the wreck of human life is made whole. No more need anyone say, 'I have been spoiled and I am waste'. There is a Saviour in the field of blood. Every day he is gathering up the wrecks to make them again. That is why we have come, brethren—have come, perhaps, hardened by a week influenced by the world and its ways—and can go away yielding to the touch of his love. And if we can feel that to be true, we shall not have come in vain.

10

THE SONS OF THUNDER
(MATTHEW 20)

THE subject of this little exhortation is that incident in Matthew 20 when Salome, the mother of Zebedee's children, came to Jesus and asked that her two sons might have positions of authority in the Kingdom of God. It seems to me that there is something in this account which has a significant connection with our presence at the breaking of bread. So I ask you to hear again the material passage and please notice carefully exactly what happened:

> "Then came to him the mother of Zebedee's children with her sons, worshipping him, and desiring a certain thing of him. And he said unto her, What wilt thou? She saith unto him, Grant that these my two sons may sit, the one on thy right hand, and the other on the left, in thy kingdom. But Jesus answered and said, Ye know not what ye ask. Are ye able to drink of the cup that I shall drink of, and to be baptized with the baptism that I am baptized with? They say unto him, We are able. And he saith unto them, Ye shall drink indeed of my cup, and be baptized with the baptism that I am baptized with: but to sit on my right hand, and on my left, is not mine to give, but it shall be given to them for whom it is prepared of my Father. And when the ten heard it, they were moved with indignation against the two brethren. But Jesus called them unto him, and said, Ye know that the princes of the Gentiles exercise dominion over them, and they that are great exercise authority upon them. But it shall not be so among you: but whosoever will be great among you, let him be your minister; and whosoever will be chief among you, let him be your servant: even as the Son of man came not to be ministered unto, but to minister, and to give his life a ransom for many." (Matthew 20:20–28)

First, notice one word in that passage—the very first word: "*Then* came to him the mother of Zebedee's children". This word connects the incident with what has gone before and puts it in context. Remember, Jesus was on his way to Jerusalem—his face was set like a flint in that direction. He seemed to be going alone, for his disciples were following at quite some distance behind and the situation between them was somewhat strained. He had told them in graphic detail what he expected to happen at Jerusalem. They were perplexed by his reference to a cross and death, and could not understand what seemed to them his melancholic obstinacy in persisting in going to the very place which was hostile towards him. In Mark's record of the same incident it says "they were amazed". What Mark meant by his word "amazed" is what we mean by being dazed: that is puzzled, befogged, filled with a sense of foreboding.

"Not mine to give"

Then came the mother of Zebedee's children, worshipping and asking that her sons John and James might sit one on the right hand and one on the left hand in Jesus' Kingdom. So we can see the situation and grasp something of the relationship which existed when Salome made her request. Let us mark this—it was the *mother* who made the request on behalf of the sons, but when Jesus made his reply he addressed it to the *sons* and not to the mother. This is evident from the fact that he used the plural pronoun in his reply: "*Ye* know not what *ye* ask; are *ye* able to drink the cup that I shall drink?" And it was the sons who answered and said, "We are able". Notice what Jesus said in reply because it was a challenge to them and to us—we must mark it well:

> "Ye shall drink indeed of my cup, and be baptized with the baptism that I am baptized with: but to sit on my right hand, and on my left, is not mine to give, but *it shall be given to them* for whom it is prepared of my Father."
>
> (verse 23)

To some extent this reply of Jesus has been misunderstood. Sometimes it has been thought that Jesus meant he had not the power nor the right to appoint to positions of authority in his Kingdom. This may have arisen because of the word "but", and then the words which follow in verse 23 which are in italics in the AV. This word translated "but" is the Greek word *alla* which means simply 'contrary'. In the account of the Transfiguration it is translated as "save": "They saw no man any more, *save* Jesus only" (Mark 9:8); that is, they saw no one *except* Jesus. Go back to Matthew 20:23, change "but" into "except", then remove the words in italics, as there is some doubt whether they were spoken by Jesus anyway, and read his reply again thus: "My cup indeed shall ye drink; but to sit on my right hand and on my left hand is not mine to give, except to those for whom it has been prepared of my Father". So Jesus is saying that it is not for him to appoint to positions of authority in his Kingdom those who are not *prepared* for it. He can appoint only those who by preparation are made worthy to occupy such positions.

Power to Appoint

We do not doubt the power and authority of Christ. At the last it will be Jesus the King who will say, "Come, ye blessed of my Father"—or "Depart from me ye cursed". "All power", he said, "is given unto me in heaven and in earth" (Matthew 28:18). So also in his reply to James and John: he has power to appoint but as a divine principle he can appoint only those who are prepared and made ready. It is not a matter of being friendly and well disposed—it goes deeper. It is a matter of being properly and adequately prepared.

Would I be right in suggesting that we are a little surprised at the reply of Jesus? We might have expected him to be more severe with the selfishness of James and John. Perhaps secretly we feel some sympathy with the ten who were indignant that these two should have sought the way to power for themselves, and that if there were some correction to be made by Jesus we feel it ought to be towards the two who made the request.

But here is the mystery. When a few moments later Jesus made a contrast between the authority of the Gentile world and the authority of his Kingdom, he was answering the indignation of the ten. And insofar as it was a correction or a rebuke, it was not directed at James and John, but more at the ten angry men who had voiced their bitterness. Although we may feel that the attitude of James and John was selfish, it seems from the reply of Jesus that there was more selfishness in the ten than there was in the two. In order to understand the motive in the request of the two and the attitude of Jesus we shall need to recollect something in the account of Mark:

> "And Simon he surnamed Peter; and James the son of Zebedee, and John the brother of James; and he surnamed them Boanerges, which is, The sons of thunder." (3:16,17)

Sons of Thunder

The usual Jewish word for son is *bar* or *ben*. Simon Barjona—Simon son of Jonah; Benhur—son of Hur; Bengurion—son of Gurion; Benjamin—son of my right hand. The idea behind this particular word is the son who receives his inheritance from his father—a passing of family responsibility. But when you take to pieces the Aramaic surname "Boan-erges", the part of it which refers to 'son' has a peculiar meaning.

Exclusively it means a son who is the builder of the family and one who can use his authority to that end. That is made doubly sure by the use of the word "thunder", which in scripture is often used to express the idea of power and authority. What Boanerges really means then is 'offspring of the divine authority'.

Prophetic Surnames

Remember this surname was given by Jesus *prophetically*. It was so with Peter: "Simon he surnamed Peter". It did not describe what Peter was then, but what he would become as a result of being with Jesus. He was not a rock then—he was rash, impetuous, and vacillating—but Jesus saw in him certain capacities which, being welded together by the power of God, could become rock-like in character. Peter's weakness, mastered by the Gospel, meant he could become as strong as rock and so he did. The same is true of James and John. Jesus looked at them, looked deeply into their elemental natures, and proclaimed that mastered by the principles and values of the Kingdom of God they could become Sons of Thunder—sons of power and authority. So he surnamed them *prophetically*.

This we need to realise as we listen to them coming to him for positions of authority in his Kingdom. They were seeking that which their surname prophesied. They were saying in effect—though of course to what extent they realised it then I cannot venture to guess—'O Master, thou who didst surname us Boanerges, fulfil thy promise, and make us truly Sons of Thunder, men of authority under thy rule in thy Kingdom.' Jesus did not rebuke them for that, for he had already hinted in their surname that this would be their destiny. He was not angry with them; he did not scorn them or speak of the folly of their request. What he did was to seek to reveal their ignorance of what the request involved.

Founded on Faith

Notice first of all what their request revealed about themselves. Remember when it was. Jesus was on his way to Jerusalem and persistently declared that he was on his way to be rejected, made to suffer and be killed. Yet it was *then* that they asked for positions of authority in his Kingdom. In spite of all their trepidation, their fear, their trembling, they had an unshakeable conviction that he was King and that somehow he would come into his Kingdom and triumph over his enemies. It does seem that their request was founded on faith.

Secondly, the request revealed their heroism. Jesus said, "Are ye able to drink of the cup that I shall drink of, and to be baptised with the baptism that I am baptised with?" And they said, "We are able". What they meant was, 'We so desire the purpose and believe in it that we do not care about the possible consequences'.

Counting the Cost

Of course, it may be said that they were just foolish, that it fell too easily from the lips because they had not counted the cost. I must say that I have not found any word from Jesus about counting the cost. I know there is a passage in Luke 14 about building a tower and going out to fight a battle and the need to count the cost, but read it again carefully and I think you will discover that it is Jesus who is counting the cost and not the disciple. Jesus is saying he needs men and women of quality who will stand firm when the heat is on, rather than large numbers who may desert him when the battle thickens. So I do not think you will hear the voice of Jesus saying, 'Well, this is what being my disciple means, but of course you ought to sit down quietly and weigh it up very carefully and consider the pros and cons and think whether it seems worthwhile—and then only take it on if you think it will not involve you in any difficulty and hardship'. I am not saying that disciples ought not to understand properly what discipleship involves, but rather that heroes are not made out of people who insist on counting the cost at every turn.

It may be said, if you do not count the cost you are foolish—then Paul was foolish when he went back to Lystra after being half stoned to death; Jesus was foolish when he set his face towards Jerusalem; Abraham was foolish when he became a nomad; Noah was foolish when he built the ark in the middle of dry land; Moses was foolish when he forsook Egypt, not fearing the wrath of the king. Measured by human wisdom it may well be foolish to commit yourself without knowing all that lies ahead. Those people at the borders of the promised land justified their refusal to enter on the ground that it would be foolish: there are walled cities and giants, they said—it would be foolish to go. I remember the case of a young sister who gave up her job and went abroad to help preach the Gospel, and some said, "She is foolish". Well, Jesus will tell us in the day of unveiling.

A Place in the Kingdom

The point we are making is that true servants of Christ are not likely to be made by those who insist on always counting the cost. So if we want to criticise the Sons of Thunder let us not do it too hastily. After all, they were seeking what every one of us in our deepest heart hopes to come to—some position of authority in the Kingdom of Christ. I know we are always praying for a humble place in his Kingdom, but the truth is there are no humble places: to be there at all will be unbelievably exalted. There are no menial tasks in the service of the King.

Perhaps there have been moments in our lives when we have brooded over this page of the New Testament and in our ear a voice has whispered that perhaps one day, somehow we might become a Son of Thunder. That was their request, and if the truth be told perhaps ours would not be far away from it. Jesus accepted their faith, did not quench their heroism, but revealed in his reply their ignorance of the true method of coming to the place of authority. He said, "Ye know not what ye ask". It was not a rebuke; it was a statement of the position, and then he went on to help them understand what they were asking. "Are ye able to drink of the cup?" Then he did a wonderful thing—he admitted them into his fellowship: "My cup indeed ye shall drink". And so they did eventually. One was martyred by the sword of Herod and the other made a lonely exile on Patmos. Yes, they drank his cup and were baptised into his baptism, and in admitting them into his fellowship he taught them their responsibility if they would come to be Sons of Thunder. Mark this:

> "But Jesus called them unto him, and said, Ye know that the princes of the Gentiles exercise dominion over them, and they that are great exercise authority upon them. But it shall not be so among you: but whosoever will be great among you, let him be your minister; and whosoever will be chief among you, let him be your servant: even as the Son of man came not to be ministered unto, but to minister, and to give his life a ransom for many."
>
> (Matthew 20:25–28)

Preparation by Service

So this is the lesson: to mark the method of Jesus for coming to his places of power. This is the preparation without which the places can never be gained. Let James and John, the two, the ten, you and me and all who seek to sit in his throne, hear it solemnly. The way to authority in his Kingdom is the way of service now—the service that gives, ministers, sacrifices. The disciples of supreme power in the Kingdom are the disciples of lowliest spirit now. If you would rise at last you must stoop at first. If you would reign you must submit. If you would hold the sceptre you must first kiss it. If you would find your life you must lose it. By the word of the King the man who rules is the man who serves. Those who are remade are those who are first broken. Yes, I know you have heard it many times before—but this is the word of Christ from the page of Matthew 20: “Are ye able to drink of the cup?”

Is there a better time to answer that question than in the solemn moment of remembrance? Is not this thing we recall the finest example of the principle we have been facing? He “made himself of no reputation, and took upon him the form of a servant ... Wherefore God also hath highly exalted him, and given him a name which is above every name.” This is the greatness of the ages; the highest revelation of all our hopes and aspirations revealed once in the man of Nazareth—and please God yet to be revealed in all those who have crowned him now and hereafter. They will sit in his throne! My brethren, as we handle the emblems let us be sure of it.

11

THREE MISTAKES ABOUT CHRIST
(MARK 6)

THIS exhortation was provoked by the concluding verses in Matthew 13 about how the people of his own country misunderstood Christ. To them he was just the carpenter's son and they could not accept his wisdom and his teaching. So "they were offended in him" (verses 54–58).

I read on into Matthew 14 and discovered that King Herod made a mistake about him. He said, "This is John the Baptist; he is risen from the dead" (verse 2).

Then I read on further into Matthew 14 and discovered that his own disciples made a mistake about him. Verse 25 tells how he came near them walking on the sea when they were struggling with the storm. They thought he was a ghost, and were terrified. So it occurred to me that here we have three different kinds of people all in some way making a mistake about Christ.

"Is not this the carpenter?"

These three incidents are all collected in one chapter, Mark 6, and presented in a concise manner. "Is not this the carpenter, the son of Mary?" This was the opinion of his neighbours, the people of the village who were most closely acquainted with him in the atmosphere of village life. They knew him very well. He had grown up with them. They had seen the young boy grow into manhood until he came to be about 30 years of age. Then he left them for a little while and returned to his village as a teacher.

In the little synagogue, the people who knew him so well listened and were taken aback. They were amazed: "Whence hath this man these things?" And mark how precise they were to detail their knowledge of him: "Is not this the carpenter, the son of Mary, the brother of James, and Joses, and of Juda, and Simon? And are not his sisters here with us?" (verse 3). They went into great detail to justify that their amazement was well-founded. He had worked among them—perhaps as the only carpenter there! "Is not this *the* carpenter?" He had wrought with his hands to earn a living and to support his family. They heard his voice and his teaching in the synagogue and they could not account for it. So that we can grasp their real attitude we must notice carefully this sentence: "And they were offended at him". They stumbled over him because they could not understand him.

John the Baptist Risen?

Come to the next example in Mark 6:12–14:

> "And they (the 12 disciples) went out, and preached that men should repent. And they cast out many devils, and anointed with oil many that were sick, and healed them. And king Herod heard of him; (for his name was spread abroad:) and he said, That John the Baptist was risen from the dead, and therefore mighty works do shew forth themselves in him."

The report of Jesus was spreading all around the country and his apostles increased it by their preaching, and by the miracles they were able to perform. This fame of the man from Nazareth eventually reached the ears of King Herod, and his immediate reaction was this: "John the Baptist is risen from the dead". Let us remember that Herod had not seen Jesus. Indeed we can say that Herod never did see him until the very last hour and even then he never heard his voice. The Lord would not speak with him.

You will remember that to satisfy the vengeance of a wanton woman, Herod had beheaded John the Baptist. But it must be evident that although John was buried, there was a sense in which his presence still haunted his murderer. In the night perhaps he would awake sweating and terrified thinking of what he had done. It reminds us of Lady Macbeth crying to her bloodstained hand, "Out, damned spot!" You can cry, but words will not remove the indelible stain of murder. Herod heard about the prophet from Nazareth. He heard of the wonders done by him and in his name, and mastered by his guilty spirit and mingled with his superstitious mind said, 'John, my tormentor, is risen from the dead.' The cowardice of an immoral mind drove him to a view of Jesus which filled him with apprehension.

A Phantom on the Sea?

The third example brings us to Mark 6:45-50. Think of the details. Jesus retired into a mountain to pray, having urged his disciples to cross the Sea of Galilee to the far side. They were rowing the vessel and the wind became strong and it was contrary. They were seamen of experience but not withstanding, they were distressed. They had great respect for old Euroclydon. Now the narrative reveals that Jesus was walking across the sea to get to the other side before them so as to meet them there. He was not on the sea to catch up with them because you will notice that Mark is careful to say, he "would have passed by them" (verse 48). But when they saw him they cried out with fear. It says, "they all saw him, and were troubled". They supposed it was a spirit—that is *phantasma*—a phantom, a ghost. I think we ought to marvel at the restraint of Mark. He says they were troubled, but probably the truth is they were terrified! Something came towards them that they did not understand. Suddenly they forgot about the tossing waves and the howling wind. They were out of their mind because they were out of their measurement—it was something they could not apprehend, and could not weigh. It was an apparition and they were filled with perplexity and fear.

So there we are: three views of Christ by three different kinds of people, each having an element of truth and yet each making a serious mistake about him. If you wonder why I say each having an element of truth, let me explain.

He is the Carpenter

In seeing Jesus as the carpenter, they saw him as one of themselves. Here is something fundamental. It is the essential teaching of the New Testament. The humanity of Christ is utterly vital to our understanding of his mission and his redemption. He is "touched with the feeling of our infirmities". In great Old Testament words, "in all their affliction he was afflicted" (Isaiah 63:9). He knows our plight because he has passed through our experience. Yes he is the carpenter, the man of our humanity, the man who is truly human. He laughed at Cana, he wept at Bethany, he was thirsty at Sychar, he sweat blood in the garden. He is not a saint with a halo—he is a carpenter with a chisel.

"John whom I beheaded"

What about Herod's view of him as John? As an assumption it is wrong—Christ was not John the Baptist—but as a declaration of truth it was real. There was still a voice from heaven and it made Herod fear and quake. The word of Christ was the reiterated voice of the Baptist. John made Herod tremble and by his teaching enforced upon the king a sense of righteousness. This is no exaggeration. The record tells us that Herod heard John gladly (Mark 6:20), and that he regarded him as a just man and holy. So there is no doubt that Herod had been moved by John and had done things in response to John's word. Herod could not slip out of the awful guilt that he had executed a holy man and a prophet. The controversy was revived and made more instant when he heard the rumour about the man from Nazareth. It was the warning of John made more incisive. Remember how John began: "Repent ye: for the kingdom of heaven is at hand". Remember how Jesus began with the very same words. Yes, indeed, in that holy one of whom John was the forerunner, the spirit of John was revived and his solemn word was repeated even more strongly. No wonder Herod said John is risen from the dead.

"They supposed it had been a spirit"

Those men upon the sea said of him, 'It is an apparition, a phantom'. Let us understand why they said it. They were faced with a mystery and were overcome by fear. They saw something that they could not fully comprehend.

Let us not think too hardly of them. How difficult it is for the finite mind of humanity fully to comprehend the infinity of Christ. Which of us dare say we have understood everything about him? He still moves over the waves of life and startles men today. They catch something of his mystery but when everything has been said, he is still an enigma. The soul who claims to know him every whit has surely missed the central thing—the mystery of Christ. So what they said in their perplexity was not far from the truth. Here, then, are three mistakes about Christ all with an element of truth.

Characters Revealed

Now no doubt the question in your minds is this: where in this rather Bible-Class-style study is the exhortational element? What is the message we may take away today to help us in the coming week? Well, here is a proposal to ponder. In every case, what those people thought about Christ reveals something about themselves. Their understanding arose out of what they were. Let us put this suggestion to the test.

Think of those who said he is the carpenter. What they meant was, he is *only* the carpenter. They were not prepared to be honest enough to face the evidence—the wonders he had said and done—and admit that he was *more* than they had imagined. They were jealous of his evident superiority. They wanted to believe only that he was a peasant like themselves. Their attitude was calculated to limit him within the range of their own desire. They wanted him to be a carpenter—that and no more. To have to face the possibility that he might be a great teacher was something that upset their comfortable way of life. To think of it made them jealous and envious. And so we are told, he was not able to do many good works there because of their unbelief.

What is revealed about Herod? He feared what he heard about Jesus because he was convicted of his own impurity. He knew he was a moral coward and could not shed the guilt. He was a weak man who held power and used it to advance his own sensuality, but who at the same time could not avoid the consciousness of the awful judgement of God. He could robe himself in purple and hide himself in the carousings of his court, but he could not escape the awful conviction that he was doomed. He was a sensual man mastered by his impurity but with enough belief to know it must be paid for.

What shall we say of the seafaring disciples? This is the most difficult. They were in the way of obedience; they were doing what their Master had bidden. I think I must say that what is revealed about them is their limited faith at that time. The record says:

> "And he went up unto them into the ship; and the wind ceased: and they were sore amazed in themselves beyond measure, and wondered." (Mark 6:51)

On a very similar occasion when they were at sea and a great storm arose and they were afraid and wakened Jesus, he said, "Why are ye fearful, O ye of little faith?" (Matthew 8:26). The thing that predominated in the incident in Mark 6 was their fear. And at that time it was stronger than their faith—they were still questioning in their hearts.

What of Our Response?

Every opinion about Christ lays bare the heart that confesses it; every criticism of Christ unmasks the mind of the criticiser. So the inescapable question now confronts us: what do we make of this Christ and what does our understanding reveal about ourselves? Are you afraid of him? Can you bring yourself to believe that he will be able to present you holy and unblameable and unreproveable, or are you in doubt about the final outcome? Do you wish that his coming could be postponed to give more time for reformation? Is he but a book apparition or a character in a story? Does he ever actually come aboard in your life or is he always passing by—just passing by? Do you think of him so much as one of us, that you are not now sure whether he can be relied on to save the world as King of Kings and Lord of Lords? Does our understanding of him limit our conception of him and what he will do? Is he not able to do many mighty works here or there because of our unbelief? You see, here is a great principle! He is limited in our lives by the limitations we place upon him. One very wise man once said, Christ is able to do for us as much as we will allow. If we make him only the carpenter, he can do for us as the carpenter of Nazareth. If we make him a judge alone he will judge us at last according to our own judgement. If his coming fills us with fear, then there must be something we have retained which we ought to shed.

Here is the word of encouragement. Get back to this holy word of God. Let it become incarnate in your consciousness. Discover anew that enigmatic but loving Christ: a human life so real, so definite, so divine, so warm, so tender, so actual, so unique, that we are compelled to cry with Thomas, "My Lord and my God". Let us not be afraid of the mystery, but let us get near to this man who walks with such a majestic step through the Gospels and let us trust him with all our heart. As he walked over the waters he said "Be of good cheer: it is I; be not afraid". That is still magnificently true. In his touch there is still healing.

12

"THE LORD IS IN THIS PLACE"
(LUKE 5)

LUKE chapter 5 is especially significant for us because it throws light on the early ministry of our Lord Jesus. Just recollect what we have read so far in this Gospel. By this time he had preached to a multitude in Capernaum, he had been to Jerusalem and cleansed the temple of the polluters of God's house, and he had performed a startling miracle on the nobleman's son. His reputation had been strongly affected by these things: his fame was beginning to spread abroad.

Coming to the Lake of Gennesaret, Jesus sought refuge in two ships and asked the fishermen to put out just a little from the land so that he could preach to the crowds from a reasonable vantage point. When the preaching was over, Jesus suggested to Simon that he launch the boat out into the deep water and start fishing again.

There were two kinds of nets used by Galilean fishermen. One was a large, strong net used for deep water fishing; the other a much smaller cast net, specially suitable for shallow water. Because of the disappointing failure these fishermen had experienced fishing all night in the deep water and catching nothing, they were now attempting to retrieve this dismal situation by trying their cast nets near to the shore. That is why Jesus found them out of the boats and "washing their nets".

Now deep water nets did not need to be washed, but those used in the shallow water did, because they collected all kinds of weeds and slime and it was essential to get rid of this before putting these nets away. Mark, describing the very same occurrence (1:16), says that while Jesus walked by the Sea of Galilee he saw Simon and Andrew casting a net into the sea—confirming that they were fishing in the shallow waters with a cast net.

This information about the nets used by the fishermen is connected significantly to what follows. This man of Nazareth urged these fishermen to put back into the deep and try again. Simon agreed, it seems, reluctantly. It meant getting out the deep water nets again after they had been put away. Actually what went through Simon's mind we can only conjecture. We might have said: 'Is it right for a carpenter to tell a fisherman how to conduct his business?'

The actual words of Simon are interesting. We have from the lips of Simon a masterpiece: "At thy word I will" (Luke 5:5). The disciple who makes that principle incarnate regularly is a disciple indeed. On this occasion Simon did what Jesus asked, and the net broke with the weight of fish. So great was the weight of fish that the two boats began to sink.

What impresses me most when I read Luke 5 is the conviction of sin in Simon's mind when he experienced this miracle. He fell at Jesus' feet and said: "Depart from me; for I am a sinful man, O Lord" (verse 8). What is the connection between a startling miracle and a conviction of sin in the mind of this fisherman? As a start I want to put to you an hypothesis. There on the deck of a fish-laden sinking trawler, Simon discovered something of the nearness of God in a way that he had never realised before. The realisation of the nearness of the great Lord of Heaven and Earth—Yahweh, God of Israel—provoked in this man a sudden sense of his unworthiness; of his utter failure and of his impoverishment. "Depart from me; for I am a sinful man, O Lord".

Suddenly, in this situation—a miracle, a load of fish—a man is on his knees crying in reverent fear, "Depart from me". It was not that Simon Peter was an especial sinner. He was no doubt a faithful Hebrew, brought up in the brotherhood of Israel, anticipating the coming of the Messiah. Yet somehow, in the presence of this undiscovered nearness of God, Simon was deeply conscious of his sinfulness. The two are connected. The discovery of the nearness of God in the most unlikely situation suddenly struck through the soul of Simon.

One of the reasons that provoked me to make this proposal was this. In Genesis 28 we read about a man who had a dream, a wonderful dream, full of angelic beings. In that dream he heard a voice full of inspired promise, and in that man's awakening consciousness he said, with a voice choked with reverent fear, "Surely the LORD is in this place; and I knew it not". He was afraid and said, "How dreadful is this place! This is none other but the house of God, and this is the gate of heaven" (verses 16,17).

Let us think about the place where he was. It was at Bethel, near Luz, a place of bleakness and barrenness. It was far from Beersheba, far from the fruitful fields, far from the tree covered hills, the flowers and verdant pastures; indeed far from all the things we think of that make us conscious of God's presence. This is the mystery. In this unlikely, unexpected place, the undiscovered nearness of God was suddenly recognised. There is a counterpart here to the man on the seashore. The result was that Jacob was afraid, and said: "How dreadful is this place!"

"Woe is me!"

I am fortified in my hypothesis, because as I turn the pages of the Bible, I see this situation recurring. Isaiah had a vision of the Lord on his throne in the worshipping presence of the Seraphim, and the prophet cried out: "Woe is me! For I am undone; because I am a man of unclean lips" (Isaiah 6:1–5). Ezekiel saw "the appearance of the likeness of the glory of the LORD" (Ezekiel 1:28) and he fell on his face in reverent fear. When the barrel of meal wasted not, and the cruse of oil failed not, the widow woman of Zarephath said to Elijah, "O thou man of God, art thou come unto me to call my sin to remembrance?" (1 Kings 17:18).

Job said to the Lord God: "I have heard of thee by the hearing of the ear: but now mine eye seeth thee. Wherefore I abhor myself, and repent in dust and ashes" (Job 42:5,6). When Gabriel brought the nearness of God to Daniel the prophet, Daniel said, "I was afraid, and fell upon my face" (Daniel 8:17). In Matthew 17 there is a record of three men and the Son of God on a mountain, and a voice which said: "This is my beloved Son, in whom I am well pleased; hear ye him" (verse 5). And those men fell on their faces and were sore afraid. It does seem that a realisation of the active nearness of God in some way or another is a force in the spiritual development of God's servants. Some of those people I have mentioned said they became conscious of their sins, but all of them could have said it.

Where the nearness of God is undiscovered and unrecognised, sometimes it is associated with the very lowest condition of human failure. Think of King Belshazzar in the middle of his night of carousing and debauchery. God was near to him; so near that eventually the finger of God wrote that man's doom on the wall of his palace. Daniel described it like this: "The God in whose hand thy breath is, and whose are all thy ways, hast thou not glorified" (Daniel 5:23). The breath of Belshazzar, foul with drunkenness and obscenity, was nevertheless in the hand of God. God was near to him but the king was deaf and blind and dead.

Think of the Apostle Paul preaching to the Athenians in their ignorant worship of the unknown God. He says, "He is not far from every one of us: for in him we live, and move, and have our being" (Acts 17:27,28). Think of the rich fool who calculated his possessions with great satisfaction: "My crops", he said, "my barns", "my goods". But we know that God was near to him, because God is near every harvest that is ever gathered. There is a sense in which the nearness of God enwrapped that rich man, but he never recognised it, until at once it broke upon him in two words—"Thou fool" (Luke 12:16–21). It is a tragedy that has been repeated ten thousand times: men busy with life, watching the market, running the rat race, planning policies, reaching goals, fighting wars, building towers, unconscious of God.

"I have done wrong"

So we come back to Simon, in the presence of the man of Nazareth and his miraculous power, who discovered unexpectedly the nearness of God, and doing that was convicted of his weakness and was filled with reverence. It is not an isolated case. In Jericho I hear Zacchaeus saying that if he had done wrong he would restore fourfold. In the presence of this man of the seamless robe, he is compelled to testify in this way. At Capernaum a Roman soldier is saying, "I am not worthy that thou shouldest enter under my roof" (Luke 7:6). In the house of Simon, at the feet of the Messiah, a woman is weeping in her repentance. At Golgotha a criminal is confessing that *his* condemnation at least, is just. I tell you, in the presence of this man others are opening their secret hearts and unmasking their private motives. In the discovered nearness of God men and women are convicted about themselves.

And I too know about this nearness. When I do wrong, this seer of Galilee is there. I know it. I rise with hope in my heart. I rise with dedication in my spirit and sometimes before noon has come I have thought, "I've lied, I've lost him, I've satisfied my greed". And in my deepest heart I know he is there. I know I have done despite to the best, the kindest and the noblest. How do I know? I know it because Peter knew it. I know it because I recognise now the nearness of the Lord God Himself. I think I understand what was in Peter's mind when he said: "Depart from me; for I am a sinful man, O Lord".

Let us be sure of this. The conviction of sin which comes upon us is not forced upon us by some awful pronouncement of judgement, or by the institution of some ritual of public confession, or by driving us back to a kind of remorseful self-scrutiny from which we can never escape. It is provoked in us, I think, by the revelation of infinite love in this man's life and in this man's death. It is the clear loving kindness of this man's compassion. It is the perfect humanity of the divinest man that ever lived. The apostles have gathered it together in many a sentence: "While we were yet sinners, Christ died for us"; "We love him, because he first loved us". It is the nearness of God when we were a long way off.

This is the mystery. Simon found it, and he was surrounded by leaping fish in a sinking boat. In the sweat of anxious labour, he discovered the nearness of God. And so did Jacob in a place where there was no door at all to the Eternal—no temple, no tabernacle, no shrine. In the barren wilderness, resting on a stone, he saw the finest ladder save one that was ever erected. He said, "Surely God is in this place".

Though we understand the reason for Simon's plea, let us thank God that his prayer was refused. "Depart from me", said Simon. But the Sin-bearer never departed. The Redeemer has never departed. He may be invisible, but he is always near. I know sometimes it does not feel that he is near. When we come hot from sinning, our own spirits then feel far away from him. But it is we who have moved, not him. He never departs—unless we have misunderstood this Gospel. The high priest knows about you. He knows you are hemmed in by the things of today. In the hour of satisfaction, in the hour of disappointment, in the hour of uncertainty, in the time of fear, in the day of tragedy or of joy, he is as near as your own breath. But most of all, he is near when we say, as Simon said: "Depart from me; for I am a sinful man, O Lord".

In the moment of contrition, in the moment of confession, in the moment of bread breaking, in this moment of heart-searching, he is ready to break through a repentant soul and pronounce upon you and me the verdict of the guiltless. God grant that in this solemn celebration, where we catch something of the nearness of the Redeemer, our conviction of sin may be turned into blessed relief. Jacob once saw a ladder, and it filled him with awe; and what he saw imperfectly has come to us, perfectly revealed in this high priest of the universe—the Son of Man betwixt heaven and earth, the ladder of God. As we handle the emblems, may we know it to be true.

13

WHAT MANNER OF SPIRIT ARE YE OF? (LUKE 9)

ACTS 8 gives us inspired and graphic testimony that the Samaritan campaign was a great success. There is of course, the fact that in a way the success was already assured. We can see this from two directions. First of all, there is the spirit of the Samaritans. It is strange that people who in many ways were estranged from the Truth, when it came to them, were ready to grasp it so surely and so firmly. We might have seen this from our Lord's first visit to them recorded for us in John 4.

The Well of Sychar

Think for instance what it says of his meeting with the Samaritan woman at the well of Sychar. How would we have measured her? What would have been our judgement of her? What would we have said? 'A flippant sinner ready to enjoy a theological argument—a woman whose heart has turned to a cinder'. That is perhaps as we would have judged her. And yet this man of Nazareth found his way into that unrepentant heart and provoked in her the one article of faith she had left.

She had a very short statement of faith. She said: "I know that Messias cometh". And he told her something then that he had never told anybody else up to that time. He said, "I that speak unto thee am he". And the wonder of it is that she believed him. As you know she left her water pots and went to tell her friends. I notice there in the narrative of John 4 that she spoke in one of her replies of "Our father Jacob" (verse 12). I wonder how long it was, how many years it had been since she ever said that—"Our Father Jacob". But she was provoked by the spirit of the King in her presence.

You know what happened. She left her water pot, not stopping to drink anything presumably, so anxious was she to tell her friends and neighbours in the city. And as a result of her testimony they were stirred and eventually came at last to confess their belief. And this is the wonder of it: this is the place where no self-respecting Jew would have thought of going, and where in order to avoid going there they took the long way round. If you look on the map, instead of going down what we might call the motorways straight through the midst of Samaria, they went the long way round to avoid going through it. In that seemingly God-forsaken place, they said this about the man of Nazareth: "This is indeed the Christ, the Saviour of the world" (verse 42). Now what a splendid confession of faith that was. There is nothing in the New Testament better than that—spoken by these unbelieving people who had fallen from the Truth. "This is indeed the Christ, the Saviour of the world".

In John 4 the narrative says about our Lord: "He must needs go through Samaria" (verse 4). What of that expression "he must needs"? It means that you are not compelled to do something, but you do it in order to satisfy your own heart and your own conviction. A wife will sometimes say of her husband, 'I told him lunch would be ready straight away, and he must needs go for a walk!' Well, brethren, you understand these things. You know how it happens. It is something you have to do, not because you are compelled to but in order to satisfy your own heart. And this is how the man of Nazareth went to Samaria: "He must needs go". Others would have avoided it; this man had to go. He was compelled by compassion to go there.

Remember that he left the metropolitan life of Jerusalem. He went to that city and they listened to him, and it says he would not commit himself to them because he knew what was in man. Isn't that remarkable? In the city of God, in the very heart of Israel's religion, he came to preach, and they received him superficially. They were interested only in the miraculous and the spectacular. And he would not commit himself to them. He left and went to Samaria where no self-respecting Jew would ever go. And there was great success in the one place where you wouldn't expect it to exist. So that is the first piece of evidence—the spirit of the Samaritans.

Witnesses in Samaria

The second piece of evidence that the Samaritan campaign would be a success brings us to the great commission which the King is giving to his men as they have to face the world without him. And he is saying to them, "ye shall be witnesses unto me both in Jerusalem, and in all Judea, and in Samaria, and unto the uttermost part of the earth" (Acts 1:8). Now notice in the extending sphere of his influence by them, he takes time and care to insert that little phrase "and in Samaria". That is the place where he first reaped a harvest where harvesters never went. But he is saying to them, 'You must go. My men must go to Samaria'. And Acts 8 proves that they did and it was a great success. So we have the second promise of success in the will and the enthusiasm of the King himself, incarnate in his own men. Here are the forces, you see, which assured success. The spirit of the people and the spirit and enthusiasm of the King.

Now the next step in this little meditation is to take a closer look at Acts 8:

> "Now when the apostles which were at Jerusalem heard that Samaria had received the word of God, they sent unto them Peter and John: who, when they were come down, prayed for them, that they might receive the Holy Spirit ... And they, when they had testified and preached the word of the Lord, returned to Jerusalem, and preached the gospel in many villages of the Samaritans."
>
> (Acts 8:14,15,25)

The personal pronoun "they" in verse 25 refers of course to Peter and John. And it says that as they were returning to Jerusalem, that is as they were on the Jerusalem road out of Samaria, they preached the Gospel in many villages of the Samaritans. Evidently they were preaching as they travelled and any village on the Jerusalem road heard the good news. That is why it says they preached "in many villages"; but not all, because not all villages were on the Jerusalem road. But those that were, received the Gospel message.

Fire from Heaven

Now come with me to Luke 9:

> "And it came to pass, when the time was come that he should be received up, he stedfastly set his face to go to Jerusalem, and sent messengers before his face: and they went, and entered into a village of the Samaritans, to make ready for him. And they did not receive him, because his face was as though he would go to Jerusalem. And when his disciples James and John saw this, they said, Lord, wilt thou that we command fire to come down from heaven, and consume them, even as Elias did? But he turned, and rebuked them, and said, Ye know not what manner of spirit ye are of. For the Son of man is not come to destroy men's lives, but to save them. And they went to another village." (verses 51–56)

Notice the geographical location—on the Jerusalem road going through Samaria. They came to a village on that very road, a village which seemed to rebuff James and John and the Master. And James and John, reacting, wanted to destroy the people there by calling down lightning from heaven because they had been indifferent to the King himself. Now the King's word to them was: "Ye know not what manner of spirit ye are of. For the Son of man is not come to destroy men's lives, but to save them". So if you put together Luke 9 and Acts 8, does it not appear likely, nay I would say almost certain, that the very village they once wanted to destroy, was a village to which they came back eventually in the Samaritan campaign to save? In each case they were on the same road going through the same villages. I say therefore, it is almost certain that the very village which might have been destroyed by their vengeance—the vengeance of eternal fire, if John had had his way—by the very same man, was saved or at least heard the good news. It said in one place in Acts 8, possibly of this village, "there was great joy in that city" (verse 8), because they heard the Gospel of salvation.

"Ye know not what ... spirit ye are of"

Now here is the thing to mark. When they wanted to destroy the village with fire, it was because they had forgotten or did not know what spirit they were really of. And when they did save the village by the Gospel, it was because they had come to know what spirit they were of. In other words the spirit of the Lord was now at work in his apostles, and as a result of it they were able to save the very village they once wanted to destroy. "The Son of man is not come to destroy men's lives, but to save them".

So arising out of this situation there is a word of exhortation for ourselves. The important point to dwell on is the solemn word of the King: "Ye know not what manner of spirit ye are of". And my question by way of exhortation is this: do you know what spirit you are of? It is so important to understand this for the following reason. The supreme and abiding test of ourselves is what we are internally. In the Truth, the spirit is the reality. Whether it is good or bad, as a man thinketh in his heart so is he. We are always saying it but we hardly believe it. It is not in the occasional external things that we do that the truth about ourselves is really discovered. It is not in the carefully premeditated things that we say that our hearts are truly revealed. God does not judge men by the occasional things they do or say, but by their spirit.

Have you ever noticed that Bible characters are sometimes weakest in the very thing for which they are notably strong? Like Abraham, the supreme example of faith, who turns to a subterfuge when he thinks he may be in danger for Sarah's sake. Moses the meekest of men once loses his temper. Elijah the fearless prophet once flees in terror when he is faced with

Jezebel's wrath. Peter the man of rock-like courage is vacillating and craven when faced with the challenge of a little servant girl. And John Zebedee, the apostle of love, is wanting to call down fire from heaven upon some poor Samaritans by whom he thinks he has been rebuffed. Occasionally men fail in the very thing for which really they are notably strong. But it is rarely the case that the occasional things reveal a man's spirit. Sometimes a man of God will fall into a vulgar language and sometimes a vulgar man will speak the words of God.

Didn't the King say that every evil word that men speak, of that they shall give account in the day of judgement? No, it is not every *evil* word, but every *idle* word (Matthew 12:36). It's the idle word that is the revelation; the idle, unpremeditated, unprepared word that comes from us artlessly that really and more exactly reveals our internal spirit. And so, if I may say, you would be well advised not to form your judgement of your speaker today by the words that he has very carefully prepared for you. No—it's a very doubtful measurement, how well a man speaks. A very doubtful measurement!

The idea to ponder then is the need to look very penetratingly at our inward spirit; to answer the question 'what spirit are we of?' I know I have said it is not revealed by the occasional prepared things we do, but I want to be careful to say that it is certainly revealed by the occasional things which come upon us—that is to say, the crises. How do we behave in the unexpected crises that microcosmically reveal what we are like inside? The tests of the spirit you see, come not at the moment for which we may carefully prepare—not as a rule. If the crisis is expected and we are able to prepare for it carefully, then it is not necessarily a revelation of our inward spirit. The effect of the Truth if it is real is the bringing out of our inwardness. And the spirit is revealed therefore in adversity and prosperity; in the place of obscurity and in the place of popularity; in times of defeat or in times of victory. Among the infinitesimals of a busy life heroes are sometimes being made for God. What?—heroes in times of defeat? Yes, most positively. Men are revealed more in times of defeat perhaps than in any other time. It is in the time of defeat that men discover what spirit they are of. And my question to you today therefore is: 'Do you know it?'; 'Do you understand it?'

Have this Mind in You

So the final argument for your reformation is this: "Let this mind be in you, which was also in Christ Jesus". The whole story of the life we have come to remember is a story in essence of the revelation of the love of God. It is disinterested love; it is self-sacrificing love; it is love stronger than death; it is love mightier than the grave; it is love which will not allow anything to stand in the way of its accomplishment—because the Son of Man is not come to destroy men's lives but to save them. The Son of Man is not come to be ministered unto, but to minister. It means therefore that he will never be satisfied until the last wrong is righted and the last tear is wiped away; until the remotest Samaritan village has been encompassed by salvation. The perpetual spirit of his life is that of a man disrobing and stooping and bending and serving; and the perpetual lesson is that the man who stoops lowest at first is the man who rises highest at last. So have this mind in you which was in Christ Jesus.

The servants of the king are not charged with the mission of compelling men to submit, and if they will not submit, then to destroy them. Rather they are charged with the commission to woo men by the winsomeness of the Gospel, and if they refuse to be wooed, then patiently to persist and to return and with the spirit of the Samaritan campaign, to realize that those who sometimes seem farthest from the Kingdom of God might be at its very doors.

The True Messiah

What would you say if you were asked, 'What are the marks which assure us that Jesus is the true Messiah?' Supposing we had to prove that the man of Nazareth was really the Messiah. I suspect I know what I would be doing. I would be turning up some prophecy in the Old Testament, and I would be showing that what the Hebrew prophets said was fulfilled. Jesus was born at Bethlehem Ephratah, he lived at Nazareth, he did this, he did that, and the old prophets' words were fulfilled. That's what I would be doing. Well, those are the authenticating signs that he is not deceiving us, that he is the true Messiah. Once John the Baptist asked this very question: "Art thou he that should come or look we for another?" And our Lord answered this question. He gave the authenticating signs that he was the true Messiah. Are we not a bit surprised by his reply? He said: "Go your way, and tell John what things ye have seen and heard; how that the blind see, the lame walk, the lepers are cleansed, the deaf hear, the dead are raised, to the poor the gospel is preached"

(Luke 7:22). That was his answer. The authenticating signs that he is true are all marks of compassion. Are we not a bit surprised at his method? Of course, it was a fulfilment of prophecy because the old prophet had seen it long before. Isaiah said: "Behold my servant, whom I uphold; mine elect in whom my soul delighteth" (Isaiah 42:1). And he went on to say he shall not break the bruised reed nor quench the smoking flax. Other men will. Other men will say: 'the reed is bruised, it is no good, throw it away'. *He* is going to say: 'the reed is bruised, but it can be mended'. Other men will say: 'the flax is smoking, it is obnoxious, put it out!' *He* is going to say: 'the flax is smoking, it can be fanned into flame'. He saw the possibilities of human redemption as no other man has ever seen them. He is an incomparable Saviour.

The men who wanted to call down fire from heaven were surnamed by our Lord, Boanerges—the Sons of Thunder. You can be sure of one thing: they were not Sons of Thunder when they wanted to bring lightning on the poor Samaritans. They might have thought they were, but they weren't. The title was bestowed upon them by the King prophetically. It didn't describe what they were then, it described what they would become before long through the power of the Gospel. "Sons of Thunder" really means 'sons of authority and power'. The King saw in them capacities which, mastered by his spirit, would make them Sons of Thunder in the true sense. It was so with Simon Peter. The King surnamed him Peter the Rock. Well he wasn't a rock then. 'Rock' wasn't a fitting description for what he was then, for then he was vacillating and impetuous. But it was a description of what he would become, mastered by the spirit of his Lord. So it was with James and John. It was not that they were Sons of Thunder by calling fire upon some poor people in Samaria. They became Sons of Thunder when later on they went back, as we are told in Acts 8, and set Samaria alight by the Gospel truth. James became a pillar of the infant church and gave his life in its defence, and John, saturated with the Lord's spirit became the brother of all afflicted souls and wrote letters tremulous with the love of God. And so at last they learned what spirit they were of, and in the truest sense, became sons of authority and power.

So here we are—I bring you back to the original enquiry. What is our spirit? How are we in the deep recesses of our life? What correspondence is there between the external and the internal? If any man hath not the spirit of Christ, he is none of his. That is the supreme test. And in the final analysis, our lives are not to be tested so much by the readiness by which we give assent to a number of formulated doctrines, but by the effect that those doctrines are having on our lives. There is no such thing as abstract truth. All truth in the long run is intended to change us, to make us more like our Saviour.

So, are we, in one degree or another, aware of the spirit we are of, whether it is a failure or success? I understand the difficulties: the hypocrisies which blast our life every day; the conventions that make us false in polite society; the continued struggle which we have against the flesh mastering us and dominating us. I understand these things. So my word of exhortation then is from the heart, a heart which is travelling the road along which you are travelling, understanding all the pitfalls and the precipices, knowing of the forces which assault us, which tempt us, which lure us away from the Truth. Knowing all these things I ask you to consider, 'Do you know what spirit you are of?'—because that is the vital thing.

And so in this solemn moment of bread breaking, when every third party is excluded and you are alone with your Redeemer, he may have something to say to you. You will understand what I mean. You will know what he is saying. Your conscience will tell you what he is saying if you are honest. Something you have to do in your life, to rectify your spirit. It may be something you have got that you ought to shed, or it may be something you have lost which you will have to reclaim before he comes. Or it may be the need to bring something out into the light and recognize it for what it is and to give it its right name and repudiate it, so that your spirit may be true to him. Whatever it is, you will know. So I say, in this solemn moment, may God give you the strength to consent to what He is asking, and in consequence to take courage and continue the pilgrimage.

14

"A LIGHT INTO THE WORLD" (JOHN 12)

THINK initially of what the Bible says about light. Remember that in the realm of God, whether it be natural or spiritual, light is an elemental thing. It is primal, fundamental, essential. We read in the book of Genesis that in the beginning the earth was without form and void. But God did a fundamental thing. He said, "Let there be light", and there was light. That was not done arbitrarily, it was done essentially. It was the beginning of an unalterable process ending in life.

Light and Life

Recall what that process was. God created light; then the waters were divided; then there came life on the earth: light, water, life. This is true of the spiritual as well—the light of the Truth; the water of baptism; the coming of new life. All this emphasises that light is an essential thing in every orbit of God's activity. The Apostle Paul confirms it: "For God, who commanded the light to shine out of darkness, hath shined in our hearts" (2 Corinthians 4:6). One is a counterpart of the other. Light is the primal precursor of life.

We shall best understand the significance of light if we can understand something of the meaning of darkness. When the earth was without form and void, the record says, "darkness covered the deep". Darkness is used in the Bible to represent abject ignorance of God and His purpose. When the New Testament writer wished to describe the transition from ignorance of God to a knowledge of the Gospel, he said that God hath called us "out of darkness into his marvellous light" (1 Peter 2:9). Where the darkness persists, there is no life. John says of the loveless man who hates his brother that he "is in darkness even until now" (1 John 2:9). In Proverbs, those who leave the paths of uprightness are said to walk in ways of darkness. The final destiny of the irremediably wicked is to be cast into outer darkness. Darkness is being mastered by that which is false; it is a cruel tyranny which ends in death and corruption; it is the source of all the woes and wounds and weariness of men; it is that condition spoken of by the

Master: "But if thine eye be evil, thy whole body shall be full of darkness. If therefore the light that is in thee be darkness, how great is that darkness!" (Matthew 6:23).

God saw this tyranny of darkness and knew the remedy. He knew man wanted illumination of the mind and irradiation of his path. And so once again God did an elemental thing. He said, "Let there be light"—and the word He spake became flesh and a Light came into the world. Recall what John says in his prologue: "The true Light, which lighteth every man", was coming into the world; "And the light shined in darkness, and the darkness comprehended it not". So he came, the Light of the World, and the frontiers of darkness were flung back. He spoke of judgement on hypocrisy and men blanched with fear. He spoke of succour and salvation and they were wooed by the compassion of the speaker.

"Light shined in darkness"

It was not just a gospel of words. He felt all the agony of the widow of Nain and raised her son from the dead. He felt the dull paralysing pain of the two sisters of Bethany and gave them their brother alive. He revitalised a man's withered hand in the synagogue on the Sabbath day, because he was that kind of Saviour. Men heard his words and marvelled; they saw his good works and glorified God. He stood in their presence and was able to say, "Which of you convicteth me of sin?" They slandered him but when they did it they made themselves liars. They beheld his glory, "full of grace and truth". So the light flashed and flamed among the streets and hills of Galilee: "A light into the world." And this is what I want to bring home to you: the light cut into the darkness incisively, like a knife.

There are two great things we have come to understand about light. The first is to be found in Ephesians 5:13: "Whatsoever doth make manifest is light". Standing in the presence of the light, men see themselves as they really are—they are made manifest. Secondly, standing in the presence of the light they find God is revealed and His will is communicated. So men thereby become responsible. As we often say—and rightly—light brings responsibility.

So it was in Galilee and Judea, when the light came into the world. Standing in the presence of that light they knew their thinking was wrong, that they had departed from the centre of things, that their measurements were false and their balances out of joint—their judgement perverted. One of the noblest of them said: "Depart from me; for I am a sinful man, O Lord." In the light, men discover themselves and God and they become responsible.

The principles which underlie this are revealed most carefully by the King in a passage recorded in John 12:46–50:

> "I am come a light into the world, that whosoever believeth on me should not abide in darkness. And if any man hear my words, and believe not, I judge him not: for I came not to judge the world, but to save the world. He that rejecteth me, and receiveth not my words, hath one that judgeth him: the word that I have spoken, the same shall judge him in the last day. For I have not spoken of myself; but the Father which sent me, he gave me commandment, what I should say, and what I should speak. And I know that his commandment is life everlasting: whatsoever I speak therefore, even as the Father said unto me, so I speak."

Notice what Jesus is saying: he came into the world as the darkness-dispelling force of light. He reveals that as the darkness is dispelled, it brings salvation and it brings judgement.

Convicting Men of Sin

The next step in our understanding of a light into the world comes in John 16:7–11:

> "Nevertheless I tell you the truth; It is expedient for you that I go away: for if I go not away, the Comforter will not come unto you; but if I depart, I will send him unto you. And when he is come, he will reprove (convict) the world of sin, and of righteousness, and of judgment: of sin, because they believe not on me; of righteousness, because I go to my Father, and ye see me no more; of judgment, because the prince of this world is judged."

Our business now is to seek to understand carefully what these words mean, because it will show us again the things which are at the very centre of the Gospel and convince us of the things which ought to dominate our preaching.

First then: *The spirit "will convict the world of sin … because they believe not on me."* It is not at all necessary to go into the meaning of sin: we understand it well. Sin is lawlessness, rebellion against God, missing the mark; it is coming to the parting of the ways and choosing wrong. The Spirit here is dealing with the one central malady of life and revealing it in relation to the man of Nazareth so as to make us understand what it is really like.

"Of sin … because they believe not on me." By this there is created a new centre from which to view sin. Thus it may be

known for what it is. What I mean is this: there are people out there who are hardened and have little conviction of sin because they do not believe in the Lord Jesus Christ. If they knew him, the conviction of sin would be intensified, because his life was a perpetual dedication to all the things which are the opposite of sin. He lived in undeviating faithfulness to the throne of God. Amid the rebellion he was loyal; amid the treason he was faithful. When I see it, as it is revealed by the Holy Spirit, I know that in the fibre of my being I am undone. I see the good and desire it, but I am in the grip of paralysis. But the King tells me: "I have taken away the sin of the world". All the guilt of the past has been put away. All the paralysis of the present he is ready to energise. It means there is plenteous redemption from the penalty and pollution and power of sin. He waits to place it at my disposal and yours.

Suppose a man is suffering from a deadly disease and you bring him the one sure remedy and he refuses it and dies. You could say he died of the disease, but it is more true to say he died because he declined the remedy. So the one true Saviour is revealed—to convict men of sin, to make them realise their awful failure and to flash the light upon the all-sufficient solution and the perfect remedy.

Righteousness and Judgement

Come to the next thing: *"Of righteousness, because I go to my Father."* What did he mean? It means that in him the Holy Spirit revealed a new and supreme ideal of righteousness which will deliver us all from false conceptions of goodness. Notice the words, "because I go to my Father". It means that there was nothing in the life of Jesus which could keep him out of the Father's presence. He had walked here amid human things, in great things and small. He had laughed and enjoyed the gifts of God; he had wept. He was tempted as no man was tempted, assaulted and defamed, and yet he lived in such a way as to compel unbelieving men to confess that there was never another like him. When he said, "I go to my Father", it revealed that there was no barrier between God's holiness and his holiness. It reveals to us that true righteousness is to have such relationships with heaven as to transform all relationships on earth and make them pure and noble—to live on earth with gladness of heart and be at home with God.

Then finally, about the Spirit's conviction: *"Of judgment, because the prince of this world hath been judged"* (RV). The Spirit's revelation brings knowledge of a new understanding of judgement and a new warning of man's responsibility.

When God broke down the doors of the cold tomb and raised to life His Son, He was saying in the sight of the whole human race that this is the one alone who is acceptable to Him. So the perfect man was made the way of approach to God for all other men. As he was accepted and approved, so God's judgement against sin was proclaimed. In that moment the prince of this world was judged. The power that takes men captive was itself arrested, indicted and sentenced. But let us remember clearly that when Jesus said that the Holy Spirit's conviction reveals that the prince of this world is judged, it means that being judged his captives are set free. How often have we sung it and yet we hardly believe it: "He came to break oppression and set the captives free." The prison door is open; the enemy has been despoiled; the monster is vanquished; the Lion of Judah is triumphant. It means you are free, if you will be free.

"Be of good cheer"

What a solemn thing the Gospel is. Does it not lay bare the things we have kept in the recesses of our life? It unmasks us and makes us to be outwardly what we are inwardly. Yet though it is solemn and searching, it is the only thing worth having. You have crowned the Christ whom the Holy Spirit has revealed. You share his victory over the prince of this world. There is a remedy for the paralysis and thank God you have found it. Remember the King's words: "Let not your heart be troubled: ye believe in God, believe also in me". "Be of good cheer; I have overcome the world."

These things are at the centre of our faith. A man may know a great deal about religious things and still not be convicted of sin, righteousness and judgement. Today there are no tongues of fire, no rushing wind, no sign or voice from heaven. And yet, light has come into the world and therefore we can find strength for our weakness, wisdom for our folly, succour for our bruises and grace to help in time of need. To walk in the light is not just to admire it—it is more to surrender to it and obey it. This means that by the light that has come into the world, life will be interpreted, service will be guided, suffering will be transfigured, the Gospel will be proclaimed and destiny will be sealed.

We come with grateful hearts to remember in tokens of bread and wine the one who proclaimed himself the Light of the World.

15

THE TURNING POINT IN ACTS
(ACTS 12)

IT was as a result of having to prepare this exhortation that I realised the remarkable importance of the things recorded in Acts 12. It represents a kind of watershed in the history of the infant ecclesia of Christ. Let me just illustrate what I mean. Think of that wonderful deliverance of the Apostle Peter from prison and from the evil designs of King Herod. In verse 17 it tells us how Peter told his fellow disciples of his release:

> "But he, beckoning unto them with the hand to hold their peace, declared unto them how the Lord had brought him out of the prison. And he said, Go shew these things unto James, and to the brethren. And he departed, and went into another place."

Now that little sentence is the last you will ever hear of the Apostle Peter in the history of the church. Of course, later on you will read his letters, and in the Galatian letter you will find Paul referring to him about the difference between them over Peter's action in the presence of the Jews from Jerusalem. But this reference to him in Acts 12 is the very last—he passes now from the scene.

Another turning point is that Jerusalem as the centre of the church also passes from sight. It is true that it appears twice more—in Acts 15 as the meeting place of the church council, and in Acts 21 when Paul visited the city and as a result his life was seriously in danger. But from an administrative and operational point of view, the centre of the church now moved to Antioch. You will remember then that all the wonderful missionary journeys and preaching activities which we read about later on in the Acts, start from and return to Antioch. It became the new centre of the evangelising church. The place from which the witnesses went forth and to which they returned to prepare for further ventures.

Another great landmark in Acts 12 is the conflict between two nations—the old nation of Israel, headed by Herod Agrippa I, and the new nation of Israel, styled by Peter quoting the Old Testament, "a chosen generation, a royal priesthood, an holy nation, a peculiar people" (1 Peter 2:9). Think of that solemn moment in the history of Israel when the king said to the rulers:

> "The kingdom of God shall be taken from you, and given to a nation bringing forth the fruits thereof."
>
> (Matthew 21:43)

The ecclesia of Christ, the infant church, was that new nation, and its members were entitled to possess the Kingdom because they were manifesting its principles, realising its values and proclaiming its fact in the world. That is, they were bringing forth the fruits of the Kingdom.

Herod Agrippa

In Acts 12 these two opposing forces are in conflict—the nation which had failed, and the nation which was on probation: the one headed by Herod Agrippa, the King of the Jews, and the other headed by Peter the Apostle. This Herod was a nephew of Herod Antipas—that is the Herod who murdered John the Baptist—and he was a grandson of Herod the Great, the one who murdered the innocent children about the time of the birth of the holy child.

The Herod in Acts 12 was a strange mixture. He had lived some thirty years in Rome, so was greatly influenced by the habits of the Roman metropolis—its vice, its debauchery, its sensuality. But strangely he had a strong affinity with things Jewish. Once the Emperor Gaius was planning to set up an image of himself in the temple at Jerusalem and Herod intervened and warned him against it. Josephus says that he was a man who loved to live in Jerusalem and was very careful about the observance of the law. But we must take what Josephus says with a pinch of salt. It is thought he was biased in favour of this Herod, desiring to bolster the conception of the Jewishness of the king, because that was the way Josephus designed his history—he was intensely Jewish himself.

One thing we can say for sure is that Herod was a very proud man, concerned about his status and fond of ostentation. He was anxious to do anything he could to enhance his popularity with the Jewish people. All this is proved by the opening verses of Acts 12:

> "Now about that time Herod the king stretched forth his hands to vex certain of the church. And he killed James the brother of John with the sword. And because he saw it pleased the Jews, he proceeded further to take Peter also."
>
> (verses 1–3)

This Herod represented the organised nation of Israel. Incidentally, he was the last king of Israel. That is another reason why Acts 12 is significant. He stands for that nation which was brought into existence to manifest the government of God in the world—a nation governed by God, so that all nations could see the wonder and breadth and beauty of His government.

You know as I know, Israel insisted on having an earthly king, like other nations, and God was dethroned in their hearts. From that moment they began to descend and at last they stand here headed by their last earthly king, a man of the flesh, concerned only with himself, motivated by worldly ambition—pre-eminently a politician. He challenges the new nation. As Luke puts it, "he put forth his hands to afflict certain of the church" (RV). I want to detain you on this little phrase: "And he killed James the brother of John with the sword".

Remember who James was—he was given the name Boanerges by Jesus—a Son of Thunder (see Chapter 10). It came out of his request through his mother that he with his brother John might sit on the right hand and on the left hand of the throne of the Kingdom when Jesus reigns. We know the reply: "Ye know not what ye ask. Are ye able to drink of the cup that I shall drink of, and to be baptized with the baptism that I am baptized with?" They said "We are able". They meant well but perhaps mercifully, they did not understand. The solemn prediction of Jesus comes to pass in Acts 12: "And he killed James the brother of John with the sword".

Why James?

There are mysterious things here. Have you ever pondered this? Why did God allow James to be slain but delivered Peter? He allowed Herod his wicked will but insisted on the miraculous saving of Peter. One was taken, the other left. This has happened many times since. Somebody has been taken who seems indispensable, full of passion and energy, a bulwark and a defence. How can we understand it? The question is even harder if it involves the breadwinner in a little family or the carer in a deprived condition. The perplexed heart cries, 'Why did God do this?' I am stressing now it is not new. It was there in Acts 12. God who delivered Peter so marvellously could have delivered James superbly, but He did not. Why, we shall never know this side of the Kingdom of God. It is no good bristling, or complaining; we must learn to wait, hard as it may be. In the long run it must be right. If we concede it was wise to save Peter, it must have been wise to let James go. God knows why, we do not. Let us rest there.

Prayer without Ceasing

Then this—think of the battle lines. A dissolute king leading a degenerate nation was faced by a praying church. Herod Agrippa, playboy of Rome, a Greek by education, an Edomite by extraction was faced by Peter, a fisherman, a weak man made strong, a faithful follower of the man of Nazareth. Against an ambitious king, flashing axes, soldiers with swords there was a praying church. Focus for a moment on the praying church. There is something here which may help us. Verse 5 says "prayer was made without ceasing" (AV margin, "instant and earnest prayer was made"). I looked up the actual word used; it means 'they agonised'. As you read the account you cannot escape the conclusion that though they were praying earnestly, they prayed doubtingly. When dear Rhoda said, "Peter is at the door", they said, "Thou art mad". There can be no doubt that their prayers were sincere and they knew what they wanted and they believed God could do it, but when He did it, they were astonished.

I am not going to criticise them one whit. To tell you the truth I feel like cheering them for they have done me good. For I am like that and I am cheered to find that they were too. People who had known the Man himself were some of them. They had seen the activity of the Holy Spirit, they were very close to the source of wonderful power, but they prayed doubtingly. It gives me encouragement to realise that there were others like me who pray doubtingly—and notwithstanding received a wonderful answer. Their fervent but halting prayer was mightier than all the force of Herod and his executioners. Jesus said, "I will build my church; and the gates of hell shall not prevail against it". In Acts 12 he is true to his word.

Angelic Ministrations

The startling thing is the method God used; that is, the ministry of angels. What do you think about the ministry of angels? Not often do we think they are active in our world. We only consider them perhaps when somebody gives an address about them. I mean daily we are not conscious of their activity, yet the Bible says they are ministering spirits sent forth to minister to those who are heirs of salvation. I said that we are not conscious of their activity—the startling thing to mark is that neither was Peter. He did not know he was free until the angel had gone. He realised the result; he did not realise the method. Is there here something to ponder? The soldiers never saw the angel. Could it be that more than we think, great things happen but we never see the method? You do not have to see the manifestation to believe that "the angel of the LORD encampeth round about them that fear him". Be careful if you are tempted to say these things do not happen today. Maybe no physical chains are broken and no shut doors are opened, but the spirit of loving care that drives them is still there. This Peter once said, "He careth for you". He knew what it meant—it would be a shame if somehow we cannot believe it. So let us thank God for the angel of Acts 12 and pray earnestly, without ceasing—even if perchance we are surprised by the result. We are in good company. There was a man who said once, "Alas, my master! How shall we do?" In reply his eyes were opened and he saw the hosts of the Lord of Hosts.

Two Kings

Come back to Herod and learn a lesson. He went to the games at Caesarea and arrayed himself in silver clothing. The sun was shining and when he made his great oration, the silver flashed and glittered, and they said, "It is the voice of a god, and not of a man". Herod loved it—Josephus says he did not reject their impious flattery, but welcomed it. Notice the end: "And immediately the angel of the Lord smote him, because he gave not God the glory" (Acts 12:23). The angel that saved Peter smote Herod. Here is something to think about. Why was he smitten at this time? He had previously killed James, but there was no judgement from heaven. He had put Peter in prison with the same intention, but there was no judgement from heaven. Yet when he failed to give glory to God he was destroyed.

Let your minds go to Daniel 5. King Belshazzar is carousing with his lords and ladies, drinking from the holy vessels of the temple—an orgy of sacrilege. Daniel goes to pronounce God's judgement. He could have charged the king with immorality, bad government, sacrilege, rebellion—but he went to the heart of the matter and said:

> "The God in whose hand thy breath is, and whose are all thy ways, hast thou not glorified." (verse 23)

That night Belshazzar died. Do you not find that startling? Two kings who gave no glory to God were both smitten.

Give Glory to God

But it is not just royalty. In Romans 3 where there is a portrait of the utter failure of human nature, it finishes with this sentence: "All have sinned, and come short of the glory of God". When the final challenge goes forth to humanity before the day of enforced humiliation, this will be the challenge:

> "Fear God, and give glory to him; for the hour of his judgment is come." (Revelation 14:7)

The explanation is in Isaiah 43:

> "I have created him for my glory, I have formed him; yea, I have made him." (verse 7)

Man was made for the glory of God. He has been endowed with wonderful powers which place him at the summit of the creation—powers which enable him to have faith in God, to trust God, to serve God, so that he can give glory to his Creator. But when those powers are wasted, prostituted, spoiled, then God is robbed of His glory. Herod did it and was smitten. Belshazzar did it and was destroyed. What does it mean?

Think of the things of His natural creation—they give glory to God. "The heavens declare the glory of God; and the firmament sheweth his handywork" (Psalm 19:1). Psalm 148 tells us the same is true of trees, flowers, hail, snow, ice, animals—they reveal the glory of God in the earth. How do they do it? By being true to the law God has placed within them. On every tulip is the law of the tulip and when it breaks forth in all its splendour, it gives glory to God. When the eagle hovers on its great eagle wings in the heavens it is faithful to the law of the eagle and gives glory to God. They are what God intended them to be and they give Him glory.

Full of Grace and Truth

So we come to man and the law of manhood, once perfectly revealed in one lonely, concentric man—the man of Nazareth. What is the law of manhood? Once in the long process of the centuries, we have seen it. Once for a brief moment it flamed out in all its beauty. Once it hovered over broken humanity—the man Christ Jesus. A few, his next of kin, saw it and testified: "We beheld his glory ... full of grace and truth". His lowly obedience, even unto death resulted in God highly exalting him, "that at the name of Jesus every knee should bow ... and every tongue should confess that Jesus Christ is Lord, to the glory of God the Father." Even the life of the Son—the child of the Eternal Spirit, the Prince of Life among the dead—even his life is measured by this unchanging principle: what he did was for the glory of God the Father. You have been created for that purpose. It is the solemn purpose of your life—an approximation to the law of manhood. It is quite practical. He humbled himself and took upon him the form of a servant.

How has it been with you this week? Your powers, your wonderful powers, were they used mostly on the transient or on the eternal? It is not my business to answer that, but it is yours. I must leave it with you in this solemn moment of memorial.

As we leave Acts 12, let us take hold of the things which are eternal. James dies, Peter lives; doors open, doors shut; the opposition of kings fail, the prayer of fervent disciples triumphs; the church goes on, the gates of hell are beaten. Remember verse 24: "the word of God grew and multiplied". And the servants of God are on the highways of the Roman Empire with the Gospel of the King.

Let us be sure of one thing. It was all made possible because once, by the determinate counsel and foreknowledge of God, this man of Nazareth was bruised to death for our sakes. In this moment of bread breaking let us celebrate it with thankful hearts.

16

HELPING THE INFIRMITIES OF THE WEAK (ROMANS 15)

LET me come to the point straight away and tell you what this exhortation is about. I am concerned to awake your serious interest in Romans 15 and the first two verses:

> "We then that are strong ought to bear the infirmities of the weak, and not to please ourselves. Let every one of us please his neighbour for his good to edification."

I want to look at these words first of all strictly in the context of Romans 14 to which the words are related and then after that to make a more general application of the appeal. So first of all in its context: "We who are strong ought to bear the infirmities of the weak". Notice in chapter 14 who the weak are in the mind of the Apostle Paul. They are people with strong opinions. But more—they are people with strong opinions about things which as far as salvation is concerned, are not important. What things?—Well you know, in this case the matter of eating meat offered to idols. How did it come about that this business of eating meat was mixed up with the religious life of believing disciples?

Meat Offered to Idols

It appears that almost all meat offered for sale in butchers' shops in pagan cities like Rome, Corinth, and Ephesus had first been sacrificially dedicated to the gods of the city. It was the common practice, so that if you were invited out to a feast you would have to face this kind of problem. Indeed if you were not fussy then the meat you bought for yourself would also come into this category. Remember Paul's words in 1 Corinthians 10 about this very thing: "Whatsoever is sold in the shambles, that eat, asking no question for conscience sake" (verse 25). The Shambles—this is an old English word for meat market. To this day in the city of York they have their Shambles, and a fascinating street it is. So Paul is saying 'when you go shopping do not worry about the history of the carcass from which the butcher cuts your joint. It does not matter.' Paul says in 1 Corinthians 8:4, "we know that an idol is nothing in the world, and that there is none other God but one". He means that the idol has no reality or authenticity so that the flesh dedicated to it is not impaired in any way or contaminated spiritually. Eat it and enjoy it.

This was the understanding of the strong in the faith. But everybody was not like this. What about the weak—that is to say, those with a sensitive conscience? Remember some of the members in the ecclesia at Rome had at one time been idol worshippers. To some extent they regarded the idol as a force to be reckoned with—to be abhorred perhaps. So anything that had a connection with it was forbidden to those who had turned from idols to worship the true God and wait for His Son from heaven.

This condition Paul calls an infirmity. An infirmity is a force which weakens or enfeebles; that is why he calls them weak. Well, what is the solution? What can you do with people like this? Can I tell you what I think our solution would be? Have a good talk to them, show them how wrong they are, get them straightened out, or start a discussion class. With some people a discussion class is the answer to every problem. When God said to Noah, 'build an ark'; or to Abraham, 'get out and go'; when Potiphar's wife said to Joseph 'lie with me'—some folk would have said 'let's start a discussion class'. A good answer sometimes, but not always.

Receive the Weak

Notice what Paul says in this case: "Him that is weak in the faith receive ye ..." (Romans 14:1). Do not leave him alone, or pass him by, or forget him, or despise him for his weakness. "Receive ye" means, 'welcome him'. Notice how it goes on: "Receive ye, but not to doubtful disputations". In a modern version it reads, "but not for disputes about opinions". Fellowship is not to be based on disputing and arguing about things that are non-essentials. Nor is it right to compel your brother to adopt your opinion in order to make him acceptable. You might have expected Paul to say that the strong must make the weak see sense—but he does not. As you know he says that the strong must be very solicitous for the feelings and spiritual welfare of the weak. The strong must not exercise their rights and their freedom in such a way as to cause the weak disciple to stumble. That could happen if the weak one sees the strong one doing something which so shocks him that he is disillusioned, loses faith and leaves the Truth; or if he is emboldened to do something which in his deepest heart he feels to be wrong, but which he is encouraged to do by the example of the strong. In other words, for love's sake the strong have to be careful how they behave towards the weak:

> "But if thy brother be grieved with thy meat, now walkest thou not charitably. Destroy not him with thy meat, for whom Christ died." (Romans 14:15)
>
> "It is good neither to eat flesh, nor to drink wine, nor anything whereby thy brother stumbleth, or is offended, or is made weak." (verse 21)

Paul says the strong must not despise the weak or judge them, nor must the weak condemn the strong when they use their freedom. The important thing is this: "We then that are strong ought to bear the infirmities of the weak, and not to please ourselves." The essential thing is that every disciple belongs to God through faith and not on the basis of what he abstains from eating. The fleshly thing between the strong and the weak is to judge and despise and to accuse and to justify. But before the tribunal of Christ all such human pretensions will be of no account.

Now you may be saying to yourself—why is Paul taking up time dealing with this point when it is so inapplicable in our way of life? Nobody bothers about meat today! Well, for this reason: it teaches us one great fact of discipleship—that we are all responsible for the spiritual welfare of our brethren and sisters. We must be concerned about God's other children. We must be careful never to harm and hinder and we must be sure always to edify and build up. And the motive is for love's sake: love of God, love of the Truth, love of the family. Remember this just now:

> "Let every one of us please his neighbour for his good to edification."
>
> "Wherefore receive ye one another, as Christ also received us to the glory of God." (Romans 15:2,7)

Applications for Today

And it does have a practical application even today at the level of the Roman context. Suppose somebody has a sensitive conscience about the kind of bread we break on Sundays. Suppose they believe fervently it should be unleavened? To force them to do otherwise makes them feel disobedient and greatly disturbed. For love's sake the strong who have no such qualms ought to bear the infirmity of the weak and try to accommodate the needs of those who have this worry.

Then there is this. We must be very careful not to set at nought our brother who has a different view of something from ourselves. Remember Romans 14:10:

> "But why does thou judge thy brother? Or why dost thou set at nought thy brother? For we shall all stand before the judgment seat of Christ."

"Set at nought" is an old-fashioned expression for 'despise'; that is to scorn, to look down on, to regard as unworthy. This happens today sometimes. I have known people to be set at nought if they do not happen to believe certain things about the temptation of Christ in the wilderness, or the witch of Endor, or the purpose of prayer. According to Paul, acceptance must not rest upon absolute sameness on non-essential questions. The Apostle in Romans 14 and 15 defends the propriety of difference. Paul loved the man who differed from him just as much as he loved the man who agreed with him. There is a place for the weak and the strong and there is one fundamental thing enjoined upon both—that they act in love. No one can inconsiderately use his freedom. It is easier for the strong to adjust his ways to the weak than the other way round. The strong must be strong enough to bear the infirmities of the weak—and not to please him or her self. This is what the sentence means, as it appears to me, strictly in the context of Romans 14 and 15, and it has significance for us in the ways I have suggested.

Restoring the Weak

Come now to a more up-to-date application. It is a matter of how to deal with those who are weak, those who fail, those who get into trouble. Listen to this:

> "If a man be overtaken in a fault, ye which are spiritual, restore such an one in the spirit of meekness; considering thyself, lest thou also be tempted."
>
> (Galatians 6:1)

Notice the identity between that sentence and Romans 15:

> "If any man be overtaken in a fault"
> (that is, the weak brother or sister)
> "ye which are spiritual" (that is, the strong person)
> "restore such an one"
> (that is, bear the infirmity of the weak)
> "in the spirit of meekness"
> (parallel to "not to please ourselves")

Pleasing yourself means being pleased *with* yourself—it means feeling superior. So "in the spirit of meekness" means 'without any superior attitude'. Why is a superior attitude outlawed? Well, because of this: "considering thyself, lest thou also be tempted". You have no reason to be superior because you do not know how you would have fared, faced with the same temptation. Or more pointedly—how would you do if you were assaulted at your weakest point? Are you intact because so far you have not been tested in the way your brother was tested? Are you so far safe because you have not been tried? Obviously this is what Paul means by "lest thou also be tempted". Not one of us has any reason to feel superior—we all have every reason to be meek and understanding. It could well have been us instead of him. So, in the case of the weak brother or sister who has failed, all our efforts must be toward restoration, and furthermore carried out in a spirit of humility. Other people's failure ought to make us realise how frail we are and that we have no reason to boast.

The Spirit of Meekness

I must be honest now, my comrades, and tell you that I have very strong feelings about this. Just recently I have seen two cases where those who failed were dealt with so unsympathetically and harshly that instead of being restored they were lost altogether. The purpose of restoration was spoiled by a failure to exercise the spirit of meekness. The strong did not bear the infirmity of the weak. Of course, we all desire to act wisely in such cases—that is getting the balance right—not to be too easy so as to corrupt the Truth; not too harsh so as to destroy the fallen one.

Let us see what James says about this wisdom:

> "Who is a wise man and endued with knowledge among you? Let him shew out of a good conversation his works with meekness of wisdom. But if ye have bitter envying and strife in your hearts, glory not, and lie not against the truth. This wisdom descendeth not from above, but is earthly, sensual, devilish. For where envying and strife is, there is confusion and every evil work. But the wisdom that is from above is first pure, then peaceable, gentle, and easy to be intreated, full of mercy and good fruits, without partiality, and without hypocrisy. And the fruit of righteousness is sown in peace of them that make peace."
>
> (James 3:13–18)

At the risk of wearying you, I stress again what Paul says about the wisdom from above, which is first pure, then peaceable. He says it is gentle. Gentleness is power held in check. Think of the sea, able to destroy the strongest vessel, able to break up the sturdiest defences—but it laps over the feet of a little child in perfect safety. That is gentleness. When you could be hard and strong and demanding and able to denounce and to destroy, instead you are gentle and understanding and kind. "Full of mercy", said James and full of "good fruits". Good fruit is fruit without rottenness, without taint, without sourness. Think what it means in practical terms. Suppose there is somebody who is fit to be condemned, somebody who ought to be exposed. Are we justified in letting the truth be told; ensuring it be upheld, that it might be vindicated? James says, 'yes, of course, but be merciful because one day you will need mercy'. Perhaps his failure resulted from his Achilles heel—do you have an Achilles heel?

Notice James says "without partiality". Think what this means. Partiality is stating only one part of the argument, the part that suits your case. It is being true in one way and untrue in another. This is the reason why James says the wisdom from above is *first* pure. That is almost always taken to mean he is insisting on keeping the purity of the doctrine. That we must do this is beyond dispute—of course we must keep the doctrine pure, but 'pure' in this context does not mean that. It has to do with the exercise of wisdom in personal relationships. 'Pure' means we must be careful not to misrepresent our brother's faith or his point of view. If we do quote him, not to pick on some part that makes him appear worse than he is and leave out some part which would make him appear better. Not much good is done by upholding the Truth in one way and in order to do it having to violate it in another. The Truth is indivisible. If you mean business you cannot be true to dogma and untrue in love and mercy.

Beware Hypocrisy

Finally James says, "without hypocrisy". Hypocrisy means using high principles when it suits you, and then living on low ones when you want to; having high principles to measure your brother by and then putting them in store for yourself. These are the things to remember—being gentle, full of mercy, easy to be intreated. By this means you who are strong ought to bear the infirmities of the weak and not be too pleased about yourselves. Paul goes on: "For even Christ pleased not himself". That is, he did not insist on having his own way, but instead he bore the reproach of evil men for our sakes. Here at the moment of remembrance is the best place to examine our attitude to the weak; here in the presence of the one who was the wisdom from above—first pure then peaceable. As we are about to handle the emblems of his sacrifice for us, as we are once more reminded of how much we need his mercy, I leave you with some words which once fell from his lips on the hillside in Galilee: "Blessed are the merciful: for they shall obtain mercy".

17

PAUL—THE HUMBLE APOSTLE
(2 CORINTHIANS 11)

THERE is a sentence in 2 Corinthians 11 which is at the root of this exhortation. When I read it I was startled and provoked; it caused me to go on and find myself here today facing you with this address. The sentence is in verse 5—the words of Paul:

> "For I suppose I was not a whit behind the very chiefest apostles".

If you wonder why I was startled and provoked, this is what happened. I thought to myself, suppose somebody else had said that. Suppose for a moment that one of your brethren here had said it—or suppose I said it. If I came to you and said, 'I suppose I am not a whit behind the very best speakers in our brotherhood', how would you react? You would almost certainly say, 'He will soon run out of hat sizes—he ought to take medical advice'. Why is this so interesting? Because it bears upon one of the hardest things in discipleship—the call to be humble.

Humility

I honestly believe that humility is the most difficult thing we have to face as followers of Christ. Bear with me while I recall for you the teaching. The King said:

> "Whosoever exalteth himself shall be abased; and he that humbleth himself shall be exalted." (Luke 14:11)

Peter said:

> "Be clothed with humility: for God resisteth the proud, and giveth grace to the humble." (1 Peter 5:5)

In the Old Testament God said through Isaiah:

> "To this man will I look, even to him that is poor and of a contrite spirit, and trembleth at my word." (Isaiah 66:2)

Through Micah:

> "What doth the LORD require of thee, but to do justly, and to love mercy, and to walk humbly with thy God?"
> (Micah 6:8)

I said, suppose I had said it. Do you know something?—I would never say it. Is that because I am a humble man, meek and modest? I am sad to tell you it is not. No—the reason I would not say it is because I am too artful. I know that if I did it would harm my reputation. You would think very badly of me—you might not invite me again. Here is a confession: I know that too often my humility is contrived.

Let me illustrate this. Suppose somebody praises you for your services or achievements in the Truth. They may include speaking, or writing, or teaching, or pastoral work, or administration. In response to the praise you act humbly. You say, 'It is nothing, a poor effort really, not worthy of notice'. This is your humility being manifested. But suppose somebody else says about your service what you have said about it. Suppose they agreed with you? Suppose they say, 'It was nothing, a poor effort and not worthy of such notice, or praise'. How do you react then? I mean not outwardly, but inwardly. Do you resent it? Are you angry inwardly? Do you think it unfair? It seems to me that genuine humility would be willing for others to agree with us about what we proposed as true. What this ought to tell us is that there is a false kind of humility which it is so easy to practise and to which I know I am prone. That is what I meant by being artful.

Honest Humility

Come back to Paul and his declaration. I want to make a proposal and I hope you will follow me in it. The surest sign of modesty is the absence of mock modesty. This is at the heart of his comment. We know, especially from this epistle, that he had often to defend himself and his apostleship against the criticism of other brethren and the hostility of those who were jealous of him. This defence he calls "boasting"—and what he means is this: he insists on his divine appointment to his high calling and claims that the result of his apostleship proves its authenticity. That is why almost incidentally he lets slip the comment, "I suppose that I am not a whit behind the very chiefest apostles". This man of Tarsus is an honest man—his humility is not contrived—it is true and untarnished.

Come to another sentence which helps the argument forward. It drops out almost incidentally as did the other:

> "I withstood him to the face, because he was to be blamed." (Galatians 2:11)

You know this was spoken of the Apostle Peter. Let us be careful now. This man Peter was one of the greatest men that ever lived. If we are to criticise him let us take off our shoes in reverence. Peter was preaching no wrong doctrine. He defended the faith with his very life. I believe that Peter would have defended the liberty of the Gentiles as fervently as Paul. Peter, who first preached the Gospel to the Gentiles, was sitting down quite naturally with them at the table to eat. But when some men came down from Jerusalem—some very Jewish men—Peter stopped eating with the Gentile believers. Under the stress of Jewish conventionality he conformed to the false thinking of his visitors. It might seem a small thing and perhaps it was, but underneath there were big principles. Paul says Peter was to be blamed and told him so straightly. An apostle giving the wrong attitude is not to be excused because he is an apostle. Paul was an honest man and openly resisted his fellow apostle, because, says Paul, he was to be blamed.

Here is something to ponder: honesty is indivisible. It is no good being honest in one thing and then ready to be dishonest in another. This was the position with Paul. How could he pass by Peter's dissimulation having written the Galatian letter—a powerful description of the freedom of the believer in Christ? A man has to be true to his own way of life and his own teaching. It is a solemn thing to think about. Shall I be judged in accordance with the standards I have promulgated in my addresses? It is so easy to talk about high principles and then tend to live by low ones. Paul was an honest man—he lived by the principles he proclaimed.

I have imagined how I would have dealt with the case of Peter. I fear I would have been tempted to say nothing. After all he is my friend and he is a good man who means well. If I did have enough courage to speak out I think it would be with great circumspection. I should prefix it with careful preparation. 'Look, I quite understand the problem and you have my genuine sympathy and I hope you will understand that I would probably have done the same, but can I just mention ... for the sake of others it might be worthwhile, bearing all things in mind ...'. I have tried to imagine what I would have done in the same or similar circumstances. The point to stress now is that this humble man was also an honest man—and it ought to teach us that in the pursuit of humility, integrity is an important element. Let us put this to the test.

Avoiding Self-Deception

To be truly humble we need to be honest about ourselves. This is the capacity to see ourselves as God sees us. He knows us through and through—we can never deceive Him, though strangely we sometimes try. This is what is meant by the

Bible word 'guile'. Guile is trying to make out something is better than it really is. In Psalm 32 one of the conditions for forgiveness is: "in whose spirit is no guile". While David remained unforgiven he had been practising guile. That is, he had been pretending that his sin was not so very sinful. He had been hiding it, but with God there is no place to hide. At last Nathan would have no evasion: he said, "You are the man". Too often I want to avoid my Nathan. I give doubtful things good names to make them plausible. Too often we are glad of human admiration; we are dazzled by human glory and delighted with human approval. We are exalted in the realisation of some material advantage. We say the world is bad and then we are glad to get the most we can from it, notwithstanding. It proves the devious complexity of human nature. Now if we can be honest and admit this, it will help us to be humble. I know that somehow I am undone. Too often I take the way which is wrong. To admit it honestly could make me more ashamed and more humble.

Be done with the guile—have no more truck with the false modesty; give up the window dressing; put away the mask; be honest. Humble yourselves therefore under the mighty hand of God that He may exalt you in due course.

"He humbled himself"

Then finally let us get down to the nitty-gritty; that is the practical issues about humility. You will know already that when you make a conscious effort to be humble, somehow it has the effect of spoiling it. Like when you say 'Oh, it is nothing really'—and you are glad to be humble when you know it is not true. I think we shall all agree that humility is not just talking humbly. It is more than saying, 'in my humble way'. I want to bring you to a living example:

> "Let this mind be in you, which was also in Christ Jesus: who, being in the form of God, thought it not robbery to be equal with God: but made himself of no reputation, and took upon him the form of a servant, and was made in the likeness of men: and being found in fashion as a man, he humbled himself, and became obedient unto death, even the death of the cross. Wherefore God also hath highly exalted him, and given him a name which is above every name: that at the name of Jesus every knee should bow, of things in heaven, and things in earth, and things under the earth; and that every tongue should confess that Jesus Christ is Lord, to the glory of God the Father."
>
> (Philippians 2:5–11)

It says plainly "he humbled himself". What did Jesus do? Well, follow the phrases: "Made himself of no reputation"; "took upon him the form of a servant", and "became obedient unto death". So on the practical level he became a servant, not for his own cause and his own reputation, but for God's cause and God's purpose. And being a servant he was obedient, and when it says "unto death" it means he would let nothing interfere with his commitment to God's will.

Being a True Servant

Translate these things into our own lives and into our service and into our commitment, and what do we have? We do not have to make resolutions about being humble. We do not have to make rules about being meek. What we have to do is truly to become a servant, in God's cause. Not in any sense for ourselves but for the advancement of His business in this world—out of reverential fear, never culpably neglecting His cause. If we do that and mean it truly and faithfully we shall be humble as a divinely natural consequence—a practical application in daily life of the words, "he took upon him the form of a servant". Remember the humble disciple is obedient. It is no part of true humility to be saying, 'I know what I should do but my personal preferences must take precedence'. Humility is not found along that road.

So it seems to me that the advice is: stop trying to be humble. Start being honest and start being a servant. Learn from the sentence in 2 Corinthians 11 that false humility is the worst kind of deception. True humility is not the assumption of a shrinking attitude which says 'I cannot serve here or there because I am too humble'. It is not a prudent calculation to be lowly. It is not talking meekly. It is a life active in the cause of love and active in the service of God. Humility is unconscious meekness too committed to be worrying about reputation.

Christ Our Example

Christ's submission was not submission through weakness. It was not resignation through infirmity. It was not the meekness of human nature. The humble Christ was not passive, but active—active in the opposition to sin, active in the cause of redemption. It was not just obstinacy, for obstinacy is the lowest form of determination. It is written plainly, "He took the form of a servant". According to Jesus and Peter this quality of humility will be followed by exaltation. What we are about to celebrate is that the wonderful possibilities encapsulated in the word 'exaltation' were made sure once for all by that one who humbled himself and became obedient unto death for our sakes. So in this solemn moment of memorial, when the bread is broken, when the wine is sipped, let us think carefully what we have to say. Above all let us be honest. We are alone with the Redeemer, so there is nobody to impress. There is no third party who will hear your confession. There is no doubt that the living Christ was manifested in the great Apostle Paul. The message of this book is that he will be manifest in you. That does not mean he will make you all Pauls, but it can mean that given your submission, you will see with his eyes, feel with his heart, and be driven by his compassion.

18

"REDEEMING THE TIME" (EPHESIANS 5)

WRITING a long time ago to people living in evil days, trying to be followers of God as dear children, Paul says, 'Be careful how you use your time'. Evidently it was vital for the Ephesians—and it is vital for us too. Probably, there never was a period in the history of our community when time was so precious. When you think about it, living the life of faith is really about the right use of time. It is stating the obvious, but everybody has to do something with time. Indolent people waste it, busy people save it, bored people kill it, conductors beat it, musicians keep it, railway trains lose it—disciples are urged to redeem it.

'Redeem' may be a strange word to use about time but it is the right word because it means 'use it to the best advantage'. The word 'redeem' comes from the market place and means to make the best bargain. So to redeem time is to take every opportunity to achieve a good result. That is why Paul says "circumspectly, not as fools, but as wise". Why it is so relevant today is that never was there an age when we have so many things to help us save time, yet never was there an age when we had so little time to spare.

If there is one phrase which characterises this age it is the phrase, 'Must dash'. I hear it constantly, even from the lips of the saints. When the day comes that we have to give an account of our stewardship individually and in detail, I can well believe we shall be making our defence like this:

'Yes, I did intend to support the preaching of the Truth more, but to be honest I just did not have the time.'

'Yes, I know I ought to have helped with the Sunday School and the Youth work and I was always intending to, but somehow in the end it was shortage of time which prevented me.'

'Yes, I know I should have been at the Bible Class because it is really important—but always somehow it got crowded out and there was no time.'

> 'The pastoral work is really vital and I wanted to join in that, and I had it all planned and gave my name in as a helper, and then in the end I was beaten by lack of time.'

The nature of our society has forced this fact upon us—that living the life of faith faithfully has become a matter of the right use of our time. So when the Apostle Paul says "not as fools, but as wise", the wisdom consists of making and striking a right balance in the use of time between the things of today and the things of eternity—between the forces which are spiritual and those which are temporal. Can I remind you of the parable of the Unjust Steward? The purpose of its main teaching is fixed in one sentence:

> "The children of this world are in their generation wiser than the children of light." (Luke 16:8)

If only the disciples of Christ would put into their religion the same devotion and persistence which unbelievers put into their ordinary affairs—that is what the parable means. Have you noticed how people with an objective in the world strive, slave, agonise, drive on and persist in the quest for success, wearing themselves out. What the parable is saying is—'Would to God the children of light were as assiduous in the pursuit of holiness and service'.

Balancing the Claims

But let me dwell for a moment on the point that a balance has to be made between conflicting claims. This is true when seeking to understand the Bible. In the Bible things are sometimes written which appear to contradict. Let me give you an example. The Apostle wrote in Galatians 6:2:

> "Bear ye one another's burdens, and so fulfil the law of Christ."

But he also notes in verse 5:

> "For every man shall bear his own burden."

This can be resolved when we know that two different words are used for 'burden'—but that is another subject. The point is simply that, just as a balance has to be drawn between one passage and another in order to come to the Truth, so a balance has to be struck between the claims of ordinary life and the claims of the life of faith, in order to live the Truth truly. That really is the meaning of "redeeming the time".

The use of the word 'redeem' is telling us that the balance is not supposed to be a neat middle position, as on a pair of scales where each side is about equally weighted. 'Redeem' is telling us to use time to the best advantage: and the best advantage is strongly in favour of the cause of Christ. The paradox is that the right balance means being heavily weighted to one side. Remember, we are striking a balance between the things which are transient and the things which are eternal—and in theory we are all strongly in favour of the eternal. This is true of course in some great crisis when the Truth has to be defended at all costs, and the very principles of spiritual life are assaulted and are in jeopardy. We shall stand up and be counted. But how often does this happen? In all the years I have been in the Truth, only twice have I had to say, 'Here I am and I will take the stand and bear the consequences!' If you are waiting for that kind of situation so that you can strike a balance in favour of the eternal, you will wait half a lifetime. No, the issues are about us every day; the transient things and the eternal things are in conflict every week. We are having to make decisions as to which way we will go all the time in the daily experiences of life. Proof that this is right is to be found in the final words of the sentence, "Redeeming the time, *because the days are evil*".

"Because the days are evil"

If you had told the people of Ephesus that they were living in evil days they would have laughed. The city was prosperous, bustling, busy, rich and thriving. But Paul is telling us that there are conditions which are favourable to the advancement of temporal things, which at the same time can be disadvantageous to the saints. The point to stress now is that they were to redeem the time in the ordinary conditions of daily life in Ephesus. And the reason? "Because the days are evil", not favourable to developing the life of faith. What concerned Paul was not some great crisis once every twenty years, but the commonplace things of Ephesian life. So this is the lesson for us to learn: redeem the time. Do not let your opportunities slip by, unused and neglected.

This is a hard thing to say but I feel I have to say it. From my own experience and from my own observation, when the claims of the Truth in the ordinary affairs of ecclesial life conflict with the claims of the other things in life, too often the claims of the Truth take second place. In theory the Truth is at the top of the list, but in practice it has to take its place among a dozen other things jostling for position. Sometimes it comes out on top and sometimes it comes out further down the list. To put it plainly, sometimes it wins and sometimes it loses.

Never was there a period when time was so precious and so overworked. Why is it that with so much time being saved compared with the old days, we have so little time to spare?

Well, it is no great mystery: today we are doing so many more things. Here is a proposal. The things which take up most of our time today are:

- jobs and careers
- homes and family
- geographical isolation

Let me speak very frankly. Sometimes I detect signs of weariness among brethren and sisters because they are trying to fit in so much. Think of this situation. Both partners in a marriage are working—there is therefore less time to spend on the things of the home which have to be done. The time which used to be free for other things now has to be taken up doing the things of home and family. So the pressure builds up and something has to go. Sometimes they are the things of the Truth which have to go. People who used to come to the Bible Class do not come now because they are too tired and there is no time. Do not misunderstand me. This is not a criticism, it is an observation. I understand the problem and you have my sympathy.

Take jobs today: jobs seem to be so demanding and often are so stressful. There are some professions today which used to be reckoned ideal because, when work finished at the end of the working day, that was it and the evenings were always free. But now all that has gone. Evening work has come almost to be normal. Ought we not to offer resistance, when forces invade our lives and rob us of time which we ought to reserve for God? I know it is not easy, and of course it is a lot easier when, like me, you are retired. And again when jobs are precarious, then independence is much more difficult—I know that too. But we ought to look at it incisively to see the extent to which we are not making the most of the present because our time is taken up by the transient.

Hard Decisions

Here are some situations which have come to my notice. You will perhaps have difficulty in believing it but I can assure you they are absolutely true:

- A brother and sister in a certain meeting went away for their holiday. Now as it turned out, the date of the ecclesial business meeting occurred just two days before their holiday was due to finish, so they came home from their holiday two days early in order to be present at the meeting. Why it is so interesting is this: that the almost universal way of dealing with that problem would be to say to the recording brother: 'We are sorry but we shall have to miss the business meeting this time because we shall be away on holiday'. It would be perfectly normal for the holiday to take precedence over the business meeting. What this brother and sister did was quite exceptional; so exceptional that some people would think they were a little off beam. But what a heart-warming thing to find somebody putting Christ's cause first!

- The boss of a firm said to the employees, 'We are getting busy and shall need you on regular overtime: we suggest on Wednesday and Thursday evenings.' One man said, 'Thursdays, yes by all means, but never on a Wednesday because on that evening I have an appointment which I always keep'. That man was a rare person, but it warms the heart to think about him, a man who puts Bible Class first.
- A family had some friends not in the Truth and the friends moved and were much nearer each other. So the friends not in the Truth said, 'Now we can get together on a Sunday and go out and you can come to us—it will be lovely'. And they had to say, 'It will be lovely, but never on a Sunday because our time is fully taken up every Sunday morning and evening without fail'.
- An ecclesia needed a recording brother and the one man who could do the job lived 19 miles away in the country. He had lived in the city till he had enough money saved and then went to live in the country. He had a lovely place and was now faced with a hard decision. He gave up his country home and moved back into the city so that he could do the work of recording brother. Geographical isolation sometimes takes time and in this case the man faced it and gave up his ambition.

The only reason I draw attention to these cases is to stress that if you mean business about redeeming the time, it may well involve you in hard thinking and courageous action. But here is something to help you. When endeavouring to strike a balance there is a right place to be standing in order to take account of both worlds. The way to do it is to apply to it the teaching of the Lord Jesus; bring it to the test of this holy word of truth.

In other words we must bring to bear upon life's circumstances the principles of heaven: earthly things measured by heavenly principles. This is what the New Testament writers always do. You would expect them to bring heavenly principles to bear upon the great things of the Truth—the vital things. But they do it with quite ordinary, everyday things. Think of some examples:

> "Husbands, love your wives, even as Christ also loved the church, and gave himself for it." (Ephesians 5:25)

> "Servants ... be obedient unto your own masters ... that ye may adorn the doctrine of God your Saviour." (Titus 2:9,10)

> "Masters ... forbear threatening: knowing that your Master also is in heaven." (Ephesians 6:9)

"Though he was rich ..."

Perhaps the best example of all is in 2 Corinthians 8, in connection with being generous with money for a collection. Some people think that money is the lowest and most ordinary thing of all, but the Apostle Paul calls it a "grace" notwithstanding. He says, "See that ye abound in this grace also". And his reason for generosity is revealed in verse 9:

> "For ye know the grace of our Lord Jesus Christ, that, though he was rich, yet for your sakes he became poor, that ye through his poverty might be rich."

So when you are weighing up whether to give time to his cause or to your own things, think of what he has given for our sakes. When the call comes for loyal service to the Truth and someone says, 'Spare thyself brother'; 'spare thyself sister' (which means let somebody else bear the burden and let somebody else take the responsibility), just think that if the Lord had spared himself, then our plight would be utterly pitiable. This man measured things by a different measuring rod, different from all other men. The disciples said, "There are four months till harvest". He said, "No—the fields are already white".

May God grant that as we consider his life we may catch something of his urgency. Let us strive to redeem the time, because the days are evil; and forgetting the things that are behind, press forward and onward, to make our future sure.

19

"RISEN WITH CHRIST" (COLOSSIANS 3)

BECAUSE you understand the Bible well you will know that the resurrection of Jesus was an integral part of the great plan of atonement. If there had been no resurrection there would have been no reconciliation. That is not speculation, for the Apostle Paul says it categorically: "If Christ be not raised ... ye are yet in your sins" (1 Corinthians 15:17). If there had been no resurrection then the death of Jesus would have been the most awful tragedy of the human race, and more still, a most terrible reflection upon the government of the universe. If there be no resurrection then sin in all its naked impurity has polluted the world. The best man that ever lived was unable to stem the flood of evil. The purest has been engulfed by the vilest. The kindest has been crushed by the cruelest. If there was no resurrection, no wonder Paul said, "We are of all men most pitiable" (verse 19, RV).

Christ Risen

Thank God we are not pitiable. Men may laugh at us but they have no need to pity us, for we have discovered a joy which has eluded them. In our hearts there is no doubt about the resurrection. Peter put it in one sentence—simply and profoundly—"This Jesus hath God raised up" (Acts 2:32). It was the Jesus who died a felon's death. It means that once in the long tale of human bondage, a man assaulted and murdered by his enemies, was raised from the dead by God to be exalted to the place of universal power. The event itself is so outstanding, so unique that the significance must be incalculable. If the purpose matches the fact then it is the greatest and most significant thing that ever happened to humanity.

Forgetting for the moment the man out in the street who has no interest in the assurance of Peter—and speaking just to ourselves, those who are blood-sprinkled and chosen—what is the real significance of this great fact for ourselves?

"This Jesus hath God raised up", means three things as it appears to me:

- First, the complete approbation by God of this man's life.
- Secondly, the rejection of all other men who are unlike him.
- Thirdly, the appointment by God of this Jesus to restore those who are rejected.

When we speak of the exaltation of Christ we have coupled the ascension to the resurrection—and when Jesus ascended into heaven it means that there was nothing in him or about him that could keep him out of the presence of the Father. Remember Peter said, "therefore being by the right hand of God exalted" (Acts 2:33). Jesus was not only raised, but exalted to the place of utter perfection and untrammelled power.

Life Accepted

Others had been raised—there was the man of Bethany, there was the daughter of Jairus, there was the widow's son at Nain. But the man of Nazareth was raised *and* exalted. And it declares in the human time and the human centuries that the life which men cannot receive or will not receive, God accepted. God is saying to all men everywhere that this man is the realisation of what God meant when He said: "let us make man". This is the man of God's pattern. This man satisfies God. If you listen carefully you can catch the note of contentment in the voice of God when He audibly spoke: "This is my beloved Son, in whom I am well pleased". He was "a man approved of God among you". And when God put forth His hand—His right hand—and lifted this man out of death He was saying in the face of the whole race that this is the archetypal life which alone is acceptable in heaven.

Think of what that life was which received the approbation of heaven. It was God-centred, it was self-emptying, it was man-serving. That description embraces all the facts of Jesus' life, and I will not insult your intelligence by seeking to prove it. You know what he was like—the man of the ages.

Life Rejected

But think of the next implication. In accepting the perfect man, God rejected all the imperfection which has marred human nature. If the perfect life is God-centred, self-emptying and man-serving, think what the rejected life is like—it is self-centred, self-seeking and self-serving. And we ought to understand one thing about the rejected life: it is not comprehended only in the things which are base, mean and vulgar. It may be cultured and refined and still absolutely self-centred. That also God rejects. It is possible for us to be satisfied with a moral standard which does not satisfy God. On earth there are gradations of life which we call vulgar and refined, and with variations in between. But in heaven there are no such gradations. There is the life of Christ and an approximation to it—and there is everything else in opposition to it. Even if it is cultured and refined, if it is also self-centred and self-serving, it is rejected by God. It follows therefore that the resurrection of Jesus is a severe condemnation of all the forces which are self-satisfied and self-centred.

Finally, this has to be emphasised: God rejects the failed life by the resurrection of Jesus, so that men can be what God intended them to be—vessels of honour for His glory. He rejects it so that the marred vessels can be remade; so that the years of the cankerworm can be restored; so that the barren desert may blossom as a rose. The resurrection is the divine ratification of a new and living way, which brings healing for our wounds and hope for broken hearts. Peter said :

> "God ... begat us again unto a living hope by the resurrection of Jesus Christ from the dead." (1 Peter 1:3, RV)

The risen man is the head of a new race, the unveiling of new values, the release of new power for paralysed sinners. So this explains why Paul says to the Colossians:

> "If ye then be risen with Christ, seek those things which are above, where Christ sitteth on the right hand of God".
> (Colossians 3:1)

This thing needs to be personal and immediate. He says, "If ye then be risen with Christ ...". The solemn question is 'If not, what then?' How can you tell?

Well, I bring you back to the original measurement—are you seeking to make the new life God-centred? Is it self-emptying, is it man-serving? Is your humanity his humanity? Are your motives his? Are your impulses his? Let not this be the discussion of a theory. Take the week that has gone by. We will not for one moment dwell on that list of sensual things in Colossians 3:5: "fornication, uncleanness, inordinate affection". You will have no difficulty recognising that. Let us for the purpose of genuine helpfulness range in another direction. Think of verse 2: "Set your affection on things above, not on things on the earth". Here is the question you are compelling me to put. With what were you principally occupied during the days of last week? Think of the hours and test them by the measurement of Paul: "Set your affection on things above". What were the master questions which dominated the hours? What shall we eat and what shall we drink and wherewithal shall we be clothed? How shall we accumulate a better share of the good things on earth? How shall we minister to the comfort of our bodies? How shall we enter into that particular pleasure which gives us so much indulgent satisfaction? The important word is 'affection'. It is not the world which is so bad but the love of the world.

Supposing a man for reasons of self-esteem abstains from all the vulgar and base things of life—his choices are fastidious and his refinements are cultured and educated. But in the deep part of his life there is no upward look, no real communication with heaven in prayer, no real joy in the service of the Truth, no faithful recognition of the spiritual life. He gives no rein to his lusts, but he is a worldly man because in reality he lives as though this were the only world. His affection is for earthly things. He has not risen with Christ. He may wear the livery of discipleship, but underneath he lives in a shroud; he is still in the grave.

Restored Life in Christ

Think of the man in Christ who has risen. His master principle is a recognition that true life is spiritual. He may move every day amongst the things of time but in the deep part of him he is focussed on the things of eternity. Fundamentally, although he is mortal he knows that he has left the dust and has drawn near to Deity. He has risen with Christ. He says it not boastfully, for every day he is in conflict with the forces of his own flesh. There are days of mortification which succeed and days which fail. The old man with his deeds is not put off so easily. The painted glitter still attracts. The man who said, "That which I hate that I do", also said this: "Christ liveth in me". It means that the life of Christ is being repeated in his Apostle.

What happens and how does it come true? Think of how the New Testament speaks of the resurrection. Jesus said, "Destroy this temple and in three days I will raise it up"—and the Gospel writer adds, "he spake of the temple of his body". Paul says in Philippians 3: "who shall change our vile body that it might be fashioned like unto his glorious body". To the Corinthians he put this question: "How are the dead raised up? And with what body do they come?" Or again, "there is a natural body, and there is a spiritual body". Why is the resurrection always focussed on the body? After all man is more than body—we have come to believe that a man's mind is the central force of his life—for "as he thinketh in his heart, so is he". Why when the word of God looks forward to the day of resurrection is there no mention of the mind being raised, only the body? Because there is a sense in which the mind has been raised already. A resurrected mind is the prelude to a resurrected body.

Renewed in Mind

What is this that is written to the Romans: "Be ye transformed by the renewing of your mind"? Those who in that day have their bodies transformed will be those whose minds have already risen with Christ—who have been transformed in spirit. There is no need to beat about the bush. Your consciousness regulates your conduct and your conduct fashions your character. The truth is that those who have been transformed by the faith they have in the risen Christ are being changed in the deep recesses of their life. The mystery is that those who trust him share his life—and it masters them and changes them. The forces which were set on harming us have been fettered and repudiated. And there are new desires, new aspirations, new outlooks. It is not just admiration for the man of Nazareth. You can admire the genius of Shakespeare but you cannot share his life. You can admire the wonder of Bach but you cannot share his life. There are people who know that Christ has risen because his life is being repeated in them. Paul said: "Christ liveth in me" (Galatians 2:20). It is perfectly practical. If you believe that this life after all is but a probation and that your real vocation is not here but in the Kingdom of God, then it will affect your attitude to all the forces of this life and this world. You will not be devoted to the acquisition of wealth, the pursuit of pleasure, the grasping of status and the satisfying of ambition. You will be wooed and won by the values of the Kingdom of God; by peace and joy and love. You will be putting on bowels of mercy, kindness, humbleness of mind, meekness, longsuffering, forbearing one another and forgiving one another—for love's sake.

Paul told the Colossians that in each resurrected life a new life was being created. It happens through the forces of the Truth: through the word of God, through the power of prayer, through the effect of fellowship in the ecclesia, through the influence of God's other children. By these means the risen Christ enters into communication with the new man and step by step makes him dominant in the life of the disciple. So, progressively, the flesh becomes a servant instead of a master. A man becomes God-centred, self-emptying, man-serving.

The Empty Tomb

As we stand by the empty tomb we ought to know without any doubt that a new race has been initiated, a new life has begun. Our preaching is not vain. The risen Christ is the demonstration of the Truth we have believed and which we love. We have no need of pity; there is pardon for all and out of it comes peace. It may defy logical explanation but it cannot be denied; you are witnesses of these things. You are the testimonial; your unshakeable faith is unassailable. You prove the truth of the affirmation by the reformation of your life. You are risen with Christ. The seals are shattered, the guards are scattered. The resurrection is proof of the Gospel's truth. We may come in confidence, however spoiled, however disappointed hitherto, and because of the risen Christ we can be transformed. In your life and in the cosmic order it is the most wonderful thing in the world. God grant you may never doubt it.

May I speak at last to any soul in this house who has come today sorrowing. To those who are sad because of bereavement—and I do not mean only the bereavement of yesterday, but perhaps of many years, yet you are still sorrowing. The memory of the loved one is still strong and the loss still felt keenly. The empty tomb is God's answer to the sorrowing heart. The sting of death has been drawn. The rider on the pale horse is vanquished. This blessed assurance should soothe every wound, illuminate every dark cloud, give new hope to every endeavour. The grave is a quiet chamber for sleeping saints. So let your hearts no more be sad. Think of what life would be like without this blessed hope and thank God that the victory over death is true, wonderfully true. May God grant that in this solemn moment of bread breaking when you dwell upon the death of the Redeemer, you may draw comfort from these things.

20

"THE PILLAR AND GROUND OF THE TRUTH" (1 TIMOTHY 3)

THIS exhortation invites you to ponder the passage that occurs at the end of 1 Timothy 3. The passage is important because it reveals one of the main reasons for the writing of the letter: "how men ought to behave themselves in the house of God".

> "These things write I unto thee, hoping to come unto thee shortly: but if I tarry long, that thou mayest know how thou oughtest to behave thyself in the house of God, which is the church of the living God, the pillar and ground of the truth. And without controversy great is the mystery of godliness: God was manifest in the flesh, justified in the Spirit, seen of angels, preached unto the Gentiles, believed on in the world, received up into glory. (verses 14–16)

Nobody who means business about discipleship can be indifferent to the proposal. It may be argued that the passage does not teach us anything about behaviour in the house of God, it merely declares the need for right behaviour. I am here to say that it does teach us something and it is the purpose of this little meditation to notice it. Notice the words which follow the phrase "the house of God"—"which is the church of the living God, the pillar and ground of the truth". Then follows an analysis of the mystery of godliness.

First of all then we have a declaration about the function of the ecclesia. I am sure we all believe that the words are not dispensational. Paul is not just speaking of those few believers in Ephesus, but of the whole company of the redeemed, the aggregation of all believing souls in every place and in every age. He speaks of the totality of those who are called, blood-sprinkled and chosen—the ecclesia of the living God in the world. He says it is "the pillar and ground of the truth".

Pillar and Ground

Think of the word 'pillar'. There are two possibilities. The great pillars you see in, say, a cathedral—designed to support the roof; or alternatively a great column, elevated to make some form of declaration—like, for example, Nelson's column in Trafalgar Square, London. I believe it is this second kind of pillar Paul has in mind. There were many such in Rome and Timothy would see similar things in Ephesus: monuments designed to elevate some memorial or some philosophy. The word 'ground' refers to the thing upon which the column rests. Perhaps the right word is 'plinth'. The idea and purpose of the plinth and the pillar is that some object or some truth or fact may be elevated so that the attention of men may be drawn to it. On the embankment in London there is a great plinth and on it a column, upon which is some ancient writing making a declaration of what at one time was an important fact. As you know we call it Cleopatra's Needle. On the other hand it may be a light—like Eddystone Lighthouse. The building is a pillar erected upon a foundation, finally resting upon a rock—but the whole purpose of the elevation is the flashing of the light.

When you sail up the Hudson River to enter New York you are arrested by the Statue of Liberty. The statue elevated upon a column, resting on a plinth, looks out to sea and is intended to proclaim a great idea—that this is the land of the free. At night a light flashes on the brow of Liberty on the statue. Now thinking of all this we can come fairly to a conclusion. The ground and the pillar—the plinth and the column—are of no use apart from what they reveal.

Secondly, the statue, the light, the proclamation, are in need of the plinth and the column in order that they may be seen. There is an interdependence, an interrelationship between the column and the thing to be revealed. A column built for a statue is an empty useless thing unless the statue is placed upon it. If the lighthouse does not flash the light, it is merely an anachronism: in a sense something false and better destroyed, for it may become a snare and a delusion. When the writing on the pillar is obliterated it cannot tell its story and though it may be kept for sentimental reasons, it has ceased to have any real value. But also that statue must have the column if it is to be seen; the light must be elevated if it is to warn and illuminate; the word written must be in a position where it can be read and understood.

Proclaiming the Word

I think you will agree that the first lesson is emerging very clearly. The ecclesia is the medium which God has instituted to proclaim the Truth. The Truth is to be elevated by the ecclesia to a height at which men may see it. If the light is to cut through the darkness it must have height; if the word is to be proclaimed it must have an instrument for its proclamation.

When Paul says "of the truth", what does he mean? Well, notice what follows—the analysis of the mystery of godliness; the manifestation of God among men. In other words the Truth is embodied in a person. God's final and all-inclusive word is revealed in His Son. He is the light of the world. It is the work of the ecclesia to reveal Jesus Christ to the world—to flash the light, to proclaim the message, to announce the declaration. The pillar and the ground of truth.

When you think about it carefully the inferences are so startling. God has chosen the ecclesia, made up of human beings, to be the means of revealing His Son to the world. Just as the *purpose* of the pillar depends upon the pillar, so God depends upon the ecclesia. Jesus Christ has chosen no means of showing himself save through his own ecclesia. The great central figure of God's purpose is hidden unless the ecclesia does its work. The Light came into the world and was focussed and centralised for a little while but then passed out of human sight and is no longer shining, apart from the shining power of God's word proclaimed by God's ecclesia in the world. This was the situation in the New Testament ecclesia. So they proclaimed the word and the world was turned upside down, or more accurately, the right way up.

But let us not miss the other side of the interrelationship. The ecclesia, apart from the person of Christ, is a useless structure. If the ecclesia does not reveal the person, if the light does not flash, if the word is not proclaimed, if the character is not unveiled—then the structure itself is an empty thing. It is retained perhaps for sentimental reasons but is an anachronism; perhaps a danger itself instead of a means of salvation; a laughing stock; a voice without articulation; a sounding brass—of no use and no value.

Revealing Christ

Observe then from the word of Paul what the purpose of the ecclesia is: to reveal the Lord Jesus Christ—the mystery of Godliness, and His purpose. It is not to solve the problems of the nations, not to initiate legislation for the spread of democracy, not to advance scientific or medical research, not to enunciate moral codes. Its work is to proclaim the Gospel of the King, and his Kingdom, to call men to repentance and faith, to warn men against the danger of sin. It is a force for good which will make no truce with evil for the sake of peace or through fear of the consequences. In the midst of chaos, uncertainty and opposition, it is a force to proclaim the master principles of the Kingdom of God, and its eventual establishment in the world upon the ruins of human government at the coming of the King. To put it plainly—there is a person the world needs to see. There is a light which lost mariners need to discover. There is a famine for the word of God and men are dying for want. It is the work of the ecclesia to face the issue because *it* has the remedy.

Remember that all this is in harmony with the work of the King himself. He once said to his men: "Ye are the light of the world". He is the Light of the world but for the time being he has committed it into the hands of the ecclesia, to throw back the frontiers of darkness and illuminate the way where broken men are groping in the gloom. "Ye are the salt of the earth". He alone has the power to halt corruption, but instrumentally he has committed it into the hands of the ecclesia—his aseptic influence being used to cleanse and purify in the little world where disciples move. The ecclesia of the Living God—that is a God who is active and at work in the midst of men through His own people, chosen to be fellow workers with Him—is the pillar and the ground of truth.

Here is the word of exhortation. With all reverence does it not fill you with awe? In the final analysis it becomes a personal matter. What the ecclesia is, you collectively are. Your spirit will decide whether the ecclesia is really the pillar and the ground of truth. The proclamation is powerless to save unless it is reinforced by the lives of men and women who live as they preach. You preach the Truth but are you passionately concerned to live and walk in truth? Your preaching is sound but does your life deny it? Do not be offended, but I am compelled to say that I am amazed at the trivial reasons disciples give for tempering the Truth in their own lives. In the minds of the unsaved the message lacks force unless it has behind it the witness of souls who believe in it and have proved its power. Think of it another way. The message of pardon ought to be backed by the testimony of men and women who are pardoned. It is the pardoned man who preaches the Gospel, the man who lives in the power of God's forgiveness—the man therefore who is forever humble—the reverent man who knows in his deepest heart that he owes everything to divine grace; the man who, standing by every pool of Bethesda, is moved by the impotence of crippled humanity—the man whose motive is compelled by love.

Worthy Witnesses

Let us not beat about the bush. The person revealed to the ecclesia is proclaimed in the individual members. This assembly today is full of gifts and graces—full of skill and talent—given by God so that you may be the pillar and the ground of truth. You must therefore be careful to send into the highways and byways, into the places of commerce, into the places of professional life, into the working ways of this society, men and women who themselves love the Truth, observe the divine law and are ready to reveal to other men the love of God which has inspired it.

Let me get down to details for a moment. It has happened that sometimes disciples have had the opportunity to proclaim the Truth, but then they had to remain silent because if they had spoken they knew that their own lives would have invalidated the very words they ought to have said. The Apostle John uses an interesting expression in his second letter,

> "I rejoiced greatly that I found of thy children walking in truth, as we have received a commandment from the Father." (verse 4)

This envisages truth as extending through the wholeness of character—the allegiance of the soul to the fundamental idea of truth. Sometimes a man would do anything rather than perjure himself in a court of law and yet his whole life is a tissue of small untruths. We hate the false calumny but sometimes we are half pleased with the false praise. You see you cannot by some careful statement of theological truth make yourself true if the very habit of your life is false. The character cannot be gilded as gold by mere words if underneath it is but tinsel. Life becomes fictitious and the sorrow is that at last it will pass into your religion, and the pillar which ought to be strong and clear and true becomes an anachronism and a failure.

So in this solemn time of bread breaking there are questions we ought to be asking ourselves. Putting it bluntly, there is a person the world needs to see and the questions are these:

- Am I helping to show him to the world or is he being devalued in me?
- There are dark and troubled waters through which the mariners are being wrecked. Am I helping to flash the light across the dark deep or are these poor men and women being left to flounder through my neglect and indifference?
- There is famine for the word of God everywhere; hungry souls are dying for lack of life-giving food; am I, having the very remedy for starvation, leaving it unused and therefore impeding the work of God?

I remember once hearing a story which well illustrates the issues of this exhortation. A preacher in a remote part of the world was telling some children the story of Jesus for the very first time. He was telling them about the mercy and compassion and kindness and service of the man of Nazareth. Suddenly one girl became excited. The teacher asked what was wrong. The girl said, "I know that man about whom you speak—he lives in our street". God grant that he may live more and more in the streets of the world—and indeed in the streets of every city, through your faithfulness.

So then, when you take time and prayer and patience to lead the unsaved towards the light of the Truth, when you show the light of the world to the prevailing darkness, when you halt the spread of corruption by your aseptic influence, you may be more and more what God intended you to be—the pillar and the ground of truth. Is there a better moment than now to resolve upon a rededication of your life to this high calling? In this solemn moment of bread breaking when you are alone with your Redeemer, come what may will you resolve to show him to the little world in which you move?

21

THE PERIL OF PROCRASTINATION (HEBREWS 3)

TO come to the point straight away—there is a question which confronts us pertinently when we read Hebrews 3. It is this: 'To what extent do the solemn words of warning there have a genuine application to us today?'

Remember what the man said:

> "Take heed, brethren, lest there be in any of you an evil heart of unbelief, in departing from the living God. But exhort one another daily, while it is called Today; lest any of you be hardened through the deceitfulness of sin."
>
> (Hebrews 3:12,13)

Think of the people to whom these solemn words were first sent. They were a group of Hebrew believers who were on the verge of leaving the faith. They were encompassed by uncertainty. They had come from the old Hebrew religion into the new faith but now they were having second thoughts. They were disappointed. In the old religion they had a real temple, a visible priesthood, a holy ritual, a clear-cut law and authenticated teachers. But now no temple, no priesthood, no ritual, no written law and no official interpreters. They were uncertain; they could not make up their minds; they were in confusion. They were tempted to retrace their steps and get back to the old stability and the old certainty. It was out of this condition that the Hebrew man said, "Take heed, brethren, lest there be in any of you an evil heart of unbelief, in departing from the living God."

But this is not your situation. You are not uncertain, you are not disappointed, you are not hankering to be rid of the faith, you are not planning to retrace your steps to the old way of life. You are here today because in your deepest heart you know that this is the Truth, that this man of Nazareth is our only Saviour, that through his redeeming blood we are cleansed from our pollution and that by way of his blessed Kingdom is our redemption. There is not in you any evil heart of unbelief, but the very opposite, a heart surcharged with faith and hope, mastered by love. So the question is, does the solemn warning of Hebrews 3 have any real relevance to us today?

Personal Responsibility

I have come to say to you that, rightly understood, it does. First of all let me make what I believe is a fundamental point. The voice of God must always create in the heart of man the consciousness of responsibility. I mean we cannot read this holy word of God without being brought face to face with some moral accountability. This is the supreme difference between the voice of God and the voice of men. Let me illustrate what I mean. I believe that William Shakespeare is the prince of human poets, but I can read the tragedy of *Macbeth* and follow its moral lessons and then go out and be immoral. I can ponder the greed of Shylock in *The Merchant of Venice* and then go out and be mastered by avarice and greed. I can go through the story of *Othello* and watch with curiosity the lust of Iago and then go out and satisfy my own lust without turning a hair. Shakespeare does not bring upon me any sense of personal responsibility. But when I read this word of God it is utterly different. When it speaks I know that I am in the presence of the final voice—I cannot escape its challenge, I cannot hide from its accusation. I know that by its very nature it creates responsibility. It is the voice of God compelling me to face the truth.

So we must be very careful if we are tempted to say that these words are interesting but to us not applicable. Let us look at them carefully and try to see in what way they do have a message for us, so far removed from their original intention. Take heed brethren lest there be in any of you what follows now. Here is my suggestion. In one way these words are a warning against the peril of procrastination. That is the purpose of the little word 'Today', dignified with a capital letter (verses 7 and 8).

> "Today if ye will hear his voice, harden not your hearts, as in the provocation, in the day of temptation in the wilderness."

Of course this is a quotation from Psalm 95, referring to the time when the rebels refused to trust God in the matter of entering the good land at Kadesh Barnea. The word 'Today' is saying 'not tomorrow'—do not postpone, defer, or put off. Do it today. These Hebrews were uncertain, wavering, unstable. They were procrastinating. Let us not think they were exceptional. There is in us a tendency to postpone and defer the hard things, and to expedite and hasten the nice things. Notice what the Hebrew man said if procrastination is persisted in. He said "lest any of you be hardened". Hardening means being eventually unresponsive, untouchable, a conscience unmovable; no tears provoked, no hearts disrupted, no appeal accepted—at last a heart like a nether millstone. What happened to the procrastinating man in Luke 9 who wanted his share of the estate above all else? "Lord, suffer me first to go and bury my father" (verse 59). Of course we cannot be sure, but going on what human nature is really like when it is mastered by the transient and knowing that this man was keen and acquisitive—perhaps this was the answer, in the same Gospel:

> "One of the company said unto him, Master, speak to my brother, that he divide the inheritance with me. And he said unto him, Man, who made me a judge or a divider over you? And he said unto them, Take heed, and beware of covetousness: for a man's life consisteth not in the abundance of the things which he possesseth. And he spake a parable unto them, saying, The ground of a certain rich man brought forth plentifully: and he thought within himself, saying, What shall I do, because I have no room where to bestow my fruits? And he said, This will I do: I will pull down my barns, and build greater; and there will I bestow all my fruits and my goods. And I will say to my soul, Soul, thou hast much goods laid up for many years; take thine ease, eat, drink, and be merry. But God said unto him, Thou fool, this night thy soul shall be required of thee: then whose shall those things be, which thou hast provided? So is he that layeth up treasure for himself, and is not rich toward God." (Luke 12:13–21)

Is it not the story of a procrastinating man who at last was hardened? Why is it so important? For this reason. The central theme of the Hebrew letter is belief and unbelief, and it enforces a very strong definition of both. It reveals that belief is more than giving consent to a number of formulated doctrines. It is possible to believe intellectually all the clauses in the *Statement of Faith* and yet be lost for time and eternity. A man may believe in the existence of God and then live as though God did not exist. A man may believe that Christ rose from the dead and then live a life of death-stricken worldliness. A man may believe that Christ is soon coming and then live as though it is postponed for a thousand years. Real belief is the answer of the will to the truths to which we have assented. It is the surrender of the life to the conviction of the Truth. It is living in accordance with what we know to be orthodox.

Unbelief

How can we affirm this so confidently? Well by the word of the Hebrew letter. Remember the end of chapter 3: "They could not enter in because of unbelief". Was their unbelief a denial of the existence of God? Did they refuse to believe in the good land before them? Did they cancel their belief that they had been delivered from Egypt with mighty power? No. They refused to act upon the word of God. They would not venture upon the promise of their Lord. They said, 'Yes it is a good land, the grapes are luscious, the rivers are beautiful, it flows with milk and honey; but there are walled cities and giants, we were as grasshoppers in their sight: we had better not go, let us make a captain and go back to Egypt'. The minority report was almost the same. They said, 'Yes it is a good land, it flows with milk and honey, the grapes are luscious, the rivers are beautiful. It is true there are walled cities and giants, but with God's help we can well overcome them; let us go in and possess it'.

That is *belief*—acting in faith upon the word of God. *Unbelief* is refusing to act upon the word of God. That is why procrastination is so serious; it affects how we act, and how we act determines our belief.

Procrastination does not interfere with your conviction about the Resurrection or Baptism or the Kingdom of God or the doctrine of the Atonement or the teaching about the Second Advent. What it does is to interfere with how you respond in the light of these great doctrines. So real belief is the handing over of our life to the claim of truth; measuring all the activities of our life by the claim which the truth about the man of Nazareth makes upon us.

So this Hebrew man is telling us something vital about *unbelief*. It is to know the Truth, to hear the message, to assent to its theological accuracy, even to bow in the presence of its intellectual claim, and yet not answer its claim in the obedience of daily living. This condition followed and persisted in at last results in hardening—and procrastination is one of the forces which advances that condition. Is it not a mysterious thing. A man becomes hardened by the very truth which might have softened him; enslaved by the very forces which could have made him free. As Paul says in 2 Corinthians 2:16, the Gospel is "to the one the savour of death unto death; and to the other the savour of life unto life". It depends how you respond.

Acting Today

Observe then the importance of the little word 'Today'. It is a perpetual protest against the philosophy which encourages us to wait, to delay, to defer to a more convenient season. Most of us would be ready to admit that there are things to be done to enhance the spirit of our discipleship: here and there some reformation to be pursued, some changes to be effected, some things to be shed, some forces to be followed which could strengthen us and help us; some association which would make us better if it were ended; some pursuit which would make us ashamed if it came out into the light. It may be that we know there is something wrong with our timetable—so much time given to the transient that the time for the eternal is short-changed. Our lives are so busy, so crowded, so congested that we are weary before the Truth gets a chance. We know it must be adjusted, we know we need a firm hand on the curriculum—but somehow it is not done. We resolve, but do not. We promise, but we forget. We submit to the theory, but somehow we fail in the practice. I am able to say this because this is the story of my life. I see the clear shining of the two ways and I rest and take my ease, and this year is like last year—or worse.

Why is it like this? The answer to that is in the heart of each soul in this assembly today. I have come not to investigate your private life, thank God, but to try to illuminate this word as best I can. You will know the answer: the weights, the impediments, the wooing forces which delay. There is one thing I can say out of my own experience. I am greatly affected by guile. Guile is the force that allows us to give high sounding names to doubtful things so that we can keep them instead of shedding them. Too often I find myself saying: 'This thing is not so bad after all—it gives me a chance to understand the dark things of life as well as the bright things. There is some benefit to be found in keeping this; it may give me the chance one day to help somebody by way of warning. How can you take a stand against the world unless you have tried its strength? I will not yet do anything drastic—better to see how things work out. It's never good to act precipitately. Caution about reformation is wise—some have gone too far in their eagerness to get things changed and lived to regret it. Take time, my soul, be careful my soul, there is time yet to get it right'.

No wonder the Holy Spirit says in Psalm 32: "Blessed is the man in whose spirit is no guile"; yea, blessed indeed. And I want you to know it is all part of the process of procrastination, and this man who speaks to us today says, unchecked it will lead to hardening. You will one day lose your tears; you will one day lose your conscience; you will one day lose your sympathy; you will one day lose your compassion; you will one day lose that love which is able to fill your life with the sweet fragrance of true fellowship. So let us receive with reverence the solemn word of the Hebrew man: "Today, if ye will hear his voice, harden not your heart ... but exhort one another daily, while it is called Today".

Well that is it really. If you are thinking to yourselves, it was a very miserable exhortation, you may well have a case, but we need not finish on a miserable note. Come back to the word 'Today'. It may be a word of solemn warning but it is also a word full of hope. While it is still 'Today' everything is possible. Every sin can still be pardoned, every failure rectified, every impediment removed, every dark cloud illuminated, every weariness rested.

The word 'Today' is the gospel of immediate possibility. The voice of Christ is speaking to you. You know what he is saying, and what he is saying is bent on your redemption. It is the voice of restfulness and the voice of strength in weakness. It is the voice of grace and compassion. It is not speculation, it is not some new philosophy. It is all-sufficient power and final love. It says, "Come unto me"—as you are with your bruises and your wounds and your weariness—"and I will give you rest". So let us not parley, let us not demur, let us hear that voice 'Today'. And in this solemn moment of bread breaking when we are alone with the Saviour and every other sound is excluded, let us listen and obey.

22

LETTERS TO THE SEVEN CHURCHES (REVELATION 2,3)

I DO not know what kind of an impression the letters to the seven churches leaves upon your mind. The impressions may be many and varied—but as far as I am concerned I must confess that I am always struck by the fact that the Christian life is not a bed of roses. It calls for sterling qualities of character if it is to be real and true.

Tribulation—Kingdom—Patience

It seems to me that there are three great words in Revelation 1:9 which sum up and gather together in the noblest sense the experience which the letters to the seven churches describe: "I John, who also am your brother, and companion in tribulation, and in the kingdom and patience of Jesus Christ". "Tribulation ... kingdom ... patience". In this context "kingdom" means the supremacy and sovereignty of God and the ultimate promise of divine government in every realm of life. In this context "patience" does not mean keeping your temper under difficult circumstances, but the spirit of endurance which is prepared to hold on in faith, believing that divine sovereignty will triumph over every circumstance at last. The word "tribulation" has as its root meaning 'pressure which brings pain'. I will show you a use of it by Jesus:

> "A woman when she is in travail hath sorrow, because her hour is come: but as soon as she is delivered of the child, she remembereth no more the anguish, for joy that a man is born into the world." (John 16:21)

The word "anguish" is the same word as "tribulation" in the mouth of John. A few sentences after Jesus had used the word in the context of the labour of pain in childbirth, he used it again in respect of his disciples: "In the world ye shall have tribulation ..." (verse 33). Here then are the three great words which John uses, describing the experience of the writer and the experience of those to whom he writes: "I am thy brother and companion in tribulation ...", that is, in the endurance and travail which results at last in life.

Spirit of the Letters

Now is not this the very spirit of the letters to the churches?

- To Ephesus—in grave danger from false teachers and enduring persecutions
- To Smyrna—in tribulation, poor, suffering; some of them in prison
- To Pergamos—dwelling where Satan had his throne and where Antipas was martyred
- To Thyatira—in danger from a false prophetess and patiently enduring her evil work
- To Sardis—overwhelmed in death, where only a few were undefiled
- To Philadelphia—keeping the word and not denying the name in spite of hardship and in most difficult circumstances
- To Laodicea—made lukewarm by prosperity; the gravest of all perils which ever threatens the church of God

Notice therefore brethren, how in all these varied circumstances the faithful ones were called upon to remain faithful in spite of every difficulty and in the face of every opposition. Although feeling the pressure of circumstances and in the midst of travail, they were to remain true to the calling of their discipleship. I say brethren, through all these letters, notice the persistence of this idea. It shows us that the Christian life is no milk and water business if it is to be true. It calls for endurance and vigilance and heroism. It proclaims the need for courage and fidelity and faith. Being a disciple in the real sense is a solemn and noble thing. The story of loyal-hearted discipleship has ever been, and still is, that if a man will live Godly in this world he shall suffer tribulation. Our faith forever contradicts the philosophy of the world. If it does not, it has lost its power and its meaning. That is the persistent experience of the true church of God: to bear witness, and in the doing of it to feel the agony of loneliness and strife caused by confronting those things which are opposed to goodness and truth.

Though the world may despise it, it is a noble and exalted calling. Tribulation? Yes, possibly, but also the Kingdom and patience which are in Jesus. It is not surprising therefore to find solemn words of warning in the letters which Jesus sent to the churches. "Remember therefore from whence thou art fallen"; "else I will come quickly"; "Repent, or else"; "hold fast till I come"; "Be watchful, and strengthen the things which remain, that are ready to die"; "Hold fast which thou hast, that no man take thy crown"; "Because thou art lukewarm ... I will spue thee out of my mouth"; "Be zealous therefore and repent". Solemn words of warning. But there is a difficulty here brethren—and it is this. We cannot bring ourselves to believe that the words apply to us. I know we are always saying they do, but we hardly believe it, that is in the personal sense. We look at them with an air of detachment and say that these are messages to the church today just as truly as in the days of John—with that we are content. But we have difficulty in believing that it means *us*.

Warnings from Jude

Consider sinners, in the collective and personal sense. Brethren, I beg you to recall something we read in Jude:

> "Beloved, when I gave all diligence to write unto you of the common salvation, it was needful for me to write unto you, and exhort you that ye should earnestly contend for the faith which was once delivered unto the saints."
>
> (verse 3)

Some of the members of the church were in danger and Jude issues a solemn word of warning: "Keep yourselves in the love of God". I do not think that Jude means 'live so that God will love you'. We ought to, that is true, but I doubt if that is what he means here. God loves us though we are undeserving. He loves us though we are not always walking in His way and our hands are not always doing His work and our lips sometimes deny His goodness. He loves us still. Some men think that when we cease to behave like sons, God ceases to be a Father, but it is not true.

Think of the young son in the parable who went into a far country and wasted his father's substance on riotous living. We might say he was undeserving of love, and yet the old man was always looking over the plain with shaded eyes to see if there was any sign of the wandering boy, and when one wonderful day the prodigal son came stumbling home the father ran out to meet him and fell on his neck and kissed him and brought him home with rejoicing. No, brethren, God loves us still, though we are not worthy. What Jude means is this: 'Keep yourselves in the love of God. Seeing you are called to the unchanging love of God, live in accordance with it. Do not do anything which grieves that One who loves so constantly. Seeing you are in the love of God behave lovingly'.

And then he goes on to issue a solemn warning in the examples he brings before them of those who failed to keep themselves in the love of God. You will recall well enough who they were, but there is one strange and remarkable thing about all those examples, and I would like you to notice it, especially because we are considering whether the words of warning in the New Testament have any real application to us today. The remarkable thing is this: all those who failed were right in the heart and purpose of God. They were right in the religion and orbit of God's activity. Just think again who they were. The people of Israel—God's chosen, delivered from Egypt and sanctified; yet they sinned in the wilderness and perished. Angels—exalted ones; but they kept not their first estate and are reserved in chains of darkness. The cities of Sodom and Gomorrah—beautiful for situation in the green plain, endowed with all the values of nature; yet they failed to perceive the truth of God in all the evidence around them and gave themselves to uncleanness and perished by eternal fire. Cain—came hotfoot from making an offering to God; yet then slew his brother. Balaam—in a certain sense uttered a prophecy about Israel more wonderful than any other; and then went on to his unutterable doom. Korah—a man of the people and leader of a popular revolt; then swallowed up in his own act of folly. All these tragedies happened to those who were right in the heart of the place where the purpose of God was being outworked.

Privilege creates responsibility and responsibility unanswered issues in destruction. Keep yourselves in the love of God. If any man thinks in his heart that the solemn warnings of the New Testament, and in particular the letters to the churches, have no application for us because we are the people of God, that man might be on the very margin of the things which the holy word of God seeks to warn us against.

Brethren, come back to the great words of Revelation 1:9:

> "I John, who also am your brother, and companion in tribulation, and in the kingdom and patience of Jesus Christ, was in the isle that is called Patmos, for the word of God, and for the testimony of Jesus Christ".

Example of Israel

Dwell for a moment upon the first example that Jude sets before us: the people of God who came to their inheritance but did not enter. The positive report given by the minority of men with faith was rejected for the negative report of the faithless majority. Numbers 14 recounts the dreadful scene at Kadesh Barnea as the congregation turned on Moses and Aaron:

"But all the congregation bade stone them with stones. And the glory of the LORD appeared in the tabernacle of the congregation before all the children of Israel. And the LORD said unto Moses, How long will this people provoke me? And how long will it be ere they believe me, for all the signs which I have shewed among them?" (verses 10,11)

At this moment in their history when God wanted to give them their inheritance, He asked for courage, trust, fidelity and endurance. Yet all they thought of was the doubtful security and comfort of Egypt. The smell of the garlic was still in their nostrils. This was not an isolated incident which happened a long time ago in a remote corner of the world. It happens in every generation.

I will bring you to the equivalent of Kadesh Barnea in the New Testament, to those whose response when called to follow Christ involved delaying tactics. The response of Jesus is:

"No man, having put his hand to the plough, and looking back, is fit for the kingdom of God." (Luke 9:62)

'I will follow thee Lord, *but* ...'. It was seen at Kadesh Barnea, and now here it is on the road to Jerusalem. How often it has been used by good men to preface some reason for not holding fast to the calling of Christ. How often has some reservation been made in the following of his way: "I will follow thee Lord, but let me first bury my father"? This seemingly laudable consideration is devastatingly dismissed by the Lord. The father was clearly still living and the possible delay lengthy. Was there the material motive of first securing the inheritance? The reply of Jesus pictures the pastoral scene of cultivating the land. Ploughing is only beneficial if wholeheartedly and diligently undertaken. Half-hearted application only brings despair:

"The sluggard will not plow by reason of the cold; therefore shall he beg in harvest, and have nothing." (Proverbs 20:4)

Conversely, single-minded dedication to the task reaps rewards:

"They that sow in tears shall reap in joy. He that goeth forth and weepeth, bearing precious seed, shall doubtless come again with rejoicing, bringing his sheaves with him." (Psalm 126:5,6)

Suffering with Christ

That is the message that comes to us today from the letters to the seven churches. Brethren, do we not know it is true, deep in our secret heart? It is better to be the companion of

Jesus with all its sacrifices than to be living in ease and luxury without him. It is far, far better to be the comrade of the lonely, despised Christ now, though he never comes to wealth or this world's greatness, than to have all the pleasures of Egypt without him. It is far, far better to submit our will to his disposal than to seek to make us a new captain for ourselves and be unworthy of our inheritance. Brethren, when you look into the face of Jesus today do you not know it is better to die with him than to win any passing momentary triumph by ourselves?

Are we ready for tribulation if that should be the way of our following him? In seeking his Kingdom are we ready for patient endurance believing in the ultimate victory of his will? In the name of God I beseech you to look the Christian life squarely in the face. Seek to know it in its truest and noblest sense, as it is revealed to us today through the letters to the churches of God.

So may we be ready for that day when we, like John, shall hear behind us the voice of a trumpet and being turned to look we also shall see the Son of Man girt about the breast with a golden girdle, with feet that shine like brass burnished in the furnace, with eyes that flash as with a flame of fire, with hair white as the driven snow. May we hear the things he will say to us amid all the carnage and darkness of the world gone mad: "I was dead, and behold, I am alive …". And so I say to my brethren and sisters, 'Let us eat and drink and take courage'.

23

THE BREAKING OF BREAD (REVELATION 21, 22)

AS a start today, think of those wonderful things we have just read about in Revelation 21 and 22. Just read them again and ponder them:

"And I John saw the holy city, new Jerusalem, coming down from God out of heaven, prepared as a bride adorned for her husband. And I heard a great voice out of heaven saying, Behold, the tabernacle of God is with men, and he will dwell with them, and they shall be his people, and God himself shall be with them, and be their God. And God shall wipe away all tears from their eyes; and there shall be no more death, neither sorrow, nor crying, neither shall there be any more pain: for the former things are passed away." (Revelation 21:2–4)

"And he shewed me a pure river of water of life, clear as crystal, proceeding out of the throne of God and of the Lamb. In the midst of the street of it, and on either side of the river, was there the tree of life, which bare twelve manner of fruits, and yielded her fruit every month: and the leaves of the tree were for the healing of the nations. And there shall be no more curse: but the throne of God and of the Lamb shall be in it; and his servants shall serve him: And they shall see his face; and his name shall be in their foreheads." (Revelation 22:1–4)

These things are the fullest realisation of all our hopes and aspirations. They are the very pole star of all our longing. They are the things that nerve us in the day of battle and sustain in times of stress and strain. Ever since our community was born brethren and sisters have looked forward and onward to the day of emancipation: the new heavens and the new earth wherein will dwell righteousness.

When I was a very new brother over fifty years ago, I remember old brethren and sisters weeping with joy when they told me about it and as they longed for it. Without doubt the vision on the distant boundary has been the one thing which has encouraged and sustained us in the involutions and the convolutions of the life of faith. Through good times and bad we have never lost our great hope: the Kingdom of God.

Now the thing I want to stress is that all these wonderful things have been made possible by the very thing we have come to celebrate—the bruising to death of the Son, the only begotten; the sacrifice of the virgin-born for love's sake. He has broken down the gates of the prison. He has cut the bars asunder. God gave him for our sakes.

A Great Privilege

This act of remembrance then is a vital part of the life of discipleship. It is the very deepest expression of fellowship. To be in the fellowship of the redeemed is a great privilege. In our community the central expression of that fellowship is to share the breaking of bread service. It is the first and final measurement of being in fellowship. When people are out of fellowship, it is that from which they are excluded. To celebrate the Lord's Supper is to celebrate the fellowship of the saints. It is a very solemn thing this celebration. We are touching holy forces. To do it wrongly and undiscerningly could bring serious judgement.

I must tell you that I am at times saddened by the easy way in which it can be treated by us. Too often I fear transient things are allowed to interfere with being present at this holy assembly. How can we be deliberately spasmodic about celebrating the Lord's death for our sakes? The Good Shepherd lay down his life for the sheep. He went into conflict with the wolf. He touched the unfathomable depth of suffering—and he asks us categorically to remember it. Whatever stops us must be something very solemn and very important. If we are allowing some paltry thing to interfere with being here then we must end it without delay, lest perchance it masters us.

Personal Involvement

But the real question which the solemnity of this celebration enforces upon us is this: how can we participate in the most real sense? What does true participation really involve? How can we evaluate the real importance of this celebration in the life of faith? Remembering those wonderful things we read in Revelation, how do we adequately express our appreciation of what has been done to make them all possible? I have a theory that the best way to strengthen our appreciation of the breaking of bread service and make us more instant upon the celebration, is to deepen our personal relationship to Christ's sacrifice: to be able to feel that Christ died for us as individuals. As Paul puts it: "He loved me and gave himself for me". Of course immediately we come up against a difficulty. Whilst it is easy to say 'Christ died for me', it is difficult to feel it. Do you find it difficult? What I mean is this, Do you find it difficult honestly to feel that Christ died because of the sin you have committed; that in some way your sin is responsible for his death? To *say it* is easy, to *feel it honestly* is not easy. Put into words it amounts to this: we certainly have sinned but we never wanted Christ to die. What I am saying is that when we can feel this personal involvement in the act of atonement, our thankfulness will be greatly intensified and our desire to express it around the emblems will be strengthened. But can we really feel it?

Let me illustrate what I mean through something else. Supposing on Sunday evening at a lecture I say that all men are sinners and that includes you—you will not be offended. You will not feel that I have insulted you; you will not be angry. I predict you will not turn a hair. But supposing that when the meeting is over I come up to one of you and say that you are a sinner and put my finger on one of the sins you are alleged to have committed and accuse you of it, the chances are that your reaction will be very different. You will be angry and may well tell me to mind my own business. Why the difference in the two reactions? Because one situation is universal and the other is personal. It is one thing to feel yourself a sinner among a few million other sinners; it hardly means anything at all. It is an entirely different thing to feel yourself a lone sinner; that is a real sinner. The matter has moved from the general to the particular, from the universal to the personal.

Now this is especially true when we seek to appreciate the death of Christ. To say that he died for the sins of the world is true but it leaves us very largely unmoved. We feel no direct responsibility and therefore no direct gratitude. But let us say—nay let us feel—that in some way he died for me personally and in some way my sins condemned him and in some way my iniquity caused his death; then our appreciation must be intensified. I say it again, it is fairly easy to *say*, but very difficult to *feel* and really believe. It is unnatural, and we shudder at the thought. Honestly we are compelled to say it is not true. After all, *we* did not betray him; that was Judas. It was Peter who denied him, not us. It was Thomas who doubted him; we have believed. Those apostles it was who were weak and deserted him. It was the priests who misrepresented him. The unknown witnesses told the lies. It was

Pilate who was the coward and pronounced the sentence. Some unnamed Roman soldier drove in the nails. We did not seek to circumvent him; that was the Pharisees. We did not hinder his teaching; that was the Scribes. We have not disputed whilst he was facing danger; that was the thoughtless disciples. Although there was not one person to speak in his defence, that was not our fault. Where were Jairus and his daughter? Where were the widow of Nain and her son? Where were Martha and Mary and their brother? If there be culprits they are not us. By what possible sophistry can we be involved in the complicity? How can the guilt honestly be fastened upon us so far removed from the awful events? Was there a more reasonable argument than this? We were not there and we did nothing to cause it.

"Ye are the children of them ..."

And yet, my comrades, the scriptures insist that in some way the dying Christ felt the weight of our sins—yours and mine—the sin we committed last week in the full light of day. At the parting of the ways when we chose the way which was wrong, with our minds awake but our conscience dulled—he felt the weight of that sin. How can it be? The principles which explain it are given us by the King:

> "Woe unto you, scribes and Pharisees, hypocrites! because ye build the tombs of the prophets, and garnish the sepulchres of the righteous, and say, If we had been in the days of our fathers, we would not have been partakers with them in the blood of the prophets. Wherefore ye be witnesses unto yourselves, that ye are the children of them which killed the prophets. Fill ye up then the measure of your fathers. Ye serpents, ye generation of vipers, how can ye escape the damnation of hell?" (Matthew 23:29–33)

Notice what the king is saying: that the Pharisees of his day were guilty of the blood of Zacharias the prophet who lived in the day of Joash king of Judah and they were guilty also of the blood of righteous Abel and all the prophets who lived before Jesus came. Is there anything more unreasonable? How could they possibly be guilty? They did none of these things; they had no hand in killing the prophets, they were not even there! Yet Jesus says they were guilty and tells them why. They were the children of those who slew the prophets, not just in the ordinary sense of being their natural descendants, but children in the sense that they had inherited the very same spirit of their fathers. They were opposing God's truth and goodness now just as their forefathers had opposed it in their day. Jesus said that the Pharisees belonged to the same confederacy of evil. By their spirit they were identified with their guilty fathers:

> "That upon you may come all the righteous blood shed upon the earth, from the blood of righteous Abel unto the blood of Zacharias son of Barachias, whom ye slew between the temple and the altar." (verse 35)

This is just an illustration, but it is in this way that the New Testament views this great sin against the Son of God. It was one system of ungodliness. So it was that the dying Stephen looked upon the action of his murderers. It was not just the act of a violent mob upon one day in one lonely place. It was an outbreak of the great principle of Sin. Stephen saw in their act the resurrection of the very same spirit that had slain the prophets, opposed Moses and crucified the just one. In other words, sin became exceedingly sinful. In the words of Romans 5, sin reigned and rose against the one who was committed to destroy it.

Now it seems to me that in this way we have a responsibility for the death of the Lord Jesus. It was Caiaphas who engineered his death. It was Judas who betrayed him. It was Peter who denied him. It was the thoughtless disciples who disputed and added to his pain. These were the forces through which the deed was done; the personalities through whom the sin was manifested. Yet these people were but enlargements of ourselves. Really it was hatred, jealousy, covetousness, prejudice, self-righteousness, envy, pride, selfishness, which caused his death. Insofar as once we have been a false friend, a sceptic, a cowardly disciple, indifferent, neglectful, willing to consent to the downfall of another to save ourselves—to that degree *we* have partaken of the forces which came against him. It is true there is a sense in which once we were the children of those who came against him. I do not need to remind you that the sin we commit against our brother, we commit against Christ; that it is possible even now, according to the Hebrew writer, to crucify afresh the Son of God and put him to an open shame. Yes it was Peter who denied him, Peter and and other disciples who had disowned him through cowardice. Yes it was the apostles who disputed in the hour of his need. Yes Judas was the traitor—Judas and any other who is prepared to nurse in his life the very things which the King is fighting against. Who among us is not in some way blameworthy, measured by this measurement? He died because of our sins, yours and mine. If all other men were perfect he would need to die for us who are not. The prophet is right. He was bruised for *our* iniquities; by his stripes *we* have been healed.

Pardon for All

Now if we can really feel this to be true, I believe our thankfulness must be intensified, and we shall participate in the memorial celebration more worthily and more anxiously. We shall have to leave the children's homework; we shall have to tell the friends, never on Sunday; we shall have to have a lie in some other day. The call is so urgent, so poignant, we cannot any longer live with the occasional and the spasmodic. The love of Christ constraineth us to end our neglect.

I know it is an awful thing to contemplate that we have a responsibility for the Lord's death, but let us recall the words of the Lamb of God: "Father, forgive them; for they know not what they do". At the very centre of the memorial service there is pardon for all. That is why we need to come so often because we sin so often. We may come with all our bruises and our weaknesses and our impoverishment, because where sin abounded grace did abound more exceedingly. We may be guilty but we are not abandoned. Remember in the very moment confession is made, and as the pardon is sought, it is granted through the high priest of the universe. No voice is heard, no sign or signal from heaven, but you can be sure the pardon is full and free. The pollution is cleansed. We are acquitted. We are free. Now if you can feel this to be true, and I stress the word *feel*, then your spiritual life must be strengthened. If there is any soul in this assembly today who might have been convicted in heart about the issue we have pondered, then my dear friend, take courage and be assured He careth for you and that He will be made known to you once again and for ever, lovingly and redeemingly, in the breaking of bread. God grant that through the fellowship of the saints this may be true for us all.